Counting on Kindness

Counting on Kindness

The Dilemmas of Dependency

WENDY LUSTBADER

THE FREE PRESS
A Division of Macmillan, Inc.
NEW YORK
Collier Macmillan Canada
TORONTO
Maxwell Macmillan International
NEW YORK   OXFORD   SINGAPORE   SYDNEY

The Free Press
A Division of Macmillan, Inc.
866 Third Avenue, New York, N. Y. 10022

Collier Macmillan Canada, Inc.
1200 Eglinton Avenue East
Suite 200
Don Mills, Ontario M3C 3N1

Printed in the United States of America

printing number
1 2 3 4 5 6 7 8 9 10

Library of Congress Cataloging-in-Publication Data
Lustbader, Wendy.
    Counting on kindness : the dilemmas of dependency / Wendy
Lustbader.
        p. cm.
    Includes bibliographical references and index.
    ISBN 0-02-919515-2
    1. Dependency (Psychology)   2. Dependency (Psychology) in old age.
3. Sick—Psychology.   4. Aged—Psychology.   5. Care of the sick—
Psychological aspects.   6. Aged—Care—Psychological aspects.
7. Helping behavior.   I. Title.
BF575.D34L87   1991   90-44842
362.4—dc20   CIP

For Barry, David, and Lauren

Contents

Preface

This book explores the time of life when we are forced to depend on others for help with our daily survival. To a greater or lesser degree, we are always dependent on others, but these contacts are voluntary. We can approach or avoid other people according to our inclinations. But when we can no longer get our own groceries, prepare our own meals, or take care of other necessities on our own, we enter into a period of life that is distinct from all the others. This book highlights that distinctiveness, attempting to portray both its hardships and compensations.

The chief consequence of dependency is that we are forced to count on the kindness of others. The vulnerability aroused by this situation awakens the basic questions of our lives: Am I worthy of love and loyalty? Are people capable of true generosity, or do they live mostly for themselves? Since an accident or illness can, at any moment, remove anyone's capacity to function independently, this exploration addresses hopes and fears belonging to all of us.

Viewed one-sidedly, illness and disability are a wasteland of degradation. We see only the loss of the freedoms and satisfactions that make life bearable, and we expect disappointing answers to these questions. In the last decade, the suicide rate of people sixty-five and older in the United

States has been increasing more rapidly than that of any other age group. Asked to comment on this phenomenon, a gerontologist stated, "[Older people] are projecting what's ahead, and just don't want to go through it."[1]

I have spent most of my working hours for the last ten years listening to people in situations of dependence. My profession as a medical social worker has taken me to hospitals, nursing homes, outpatient clinics, and private homes. It turns out that there are many more dimensions to illness and disability than are encompassed by our dire images. This book is a direct reply to all who claim that little of worth happens at this time of life and that dependency is to be dreaded, no matter what the circumstances or the consolations.

The first chapter lays out the major themes to be covered in the rest of the book: feeling angry and helpless in response to dependency, making the transition from an active life to confinement, handling thoughts and reflections about the past, noticing shifts in key relationships, realizing that time is running out and options are shrinking, and finding ways to live well in spite of all of these changes. The subsequent chapters expand on each of these themes, drawing them out and identifying ways to prevail.

My hope is that this book will be passed back and forth between dependent people and those who assist them. Both sides may be relieved to recognize the universal aspects of what would otherwise be misperceived as personal pain. They may also be able to convey their feelings less hurtfully to each other through the printed page than the spoken word. Ultimately, seeing each other's position may make it easier to find a balance point in the center of chaotic emotions and unpredictable circumstances.

For those who provide care to dependent people, the

question of how much time to spend arises repeatedly. There is always something else that can be done on a dependent person's behalf. Some people let the boundaries of their own lives slip until virtually nothing remains. They take little time for themselves, and they never insist that the ill person consider their needs. It is as if they die in his or her stead, giving up whatever would have been pleasurable or life-enhancing. Others go to the opposite extreme, withdrawing from all but the most minimal tasks in a rigid effort at self-protection.

For people in need of help, the complexity reaches parallel proportions. Some surrender entirely to the whims of their helpers, believing that they have lost their entitlement to self-assertion. Others feel so degraded by the idea of being beholden to helpers that they conceal their disabilities and risk injuring themselves in order to avoid asking for help or appearing to be in need. Through surrender or concealment, they sacrifice much of what formerly made their lives worthwhile.

Often, we have to go from one extreme to the other until we find solutions to these dilemmas. With society providing fewer and fewer rules to guide those who give and receive care, the burden of choice is often more wearying than the tasks themselves. How much assistance to expect and how much to give have become private negotiations rather than culturally prescribed actions.

Throughout, I try to let the voices of people in situations of dependence be heard rather than to develop theoretical formulations. These accounts are presented in the form of vignettes, with identifying details omitted for the sake of both brevity and privacy. In some instances, I have merged the insights of several people into one, or have altered the surrounding situations, but each vignette remains

faithful to the spirit of what was told to me. Any close re-
semblance to an actual person or circumstance is therefore
coincidental.

At this writing, I am neither elderly nor disabled,
and I do not presume to know these situations in the
way that those living these circumstances know them.
Ludwig Wittgenstein, the philosopher of language, depicts
how someone entering a foreign land begins to understand
what its citizens are saying:

> Someone coming into a strange country will some-
> times learn the language of the inhabitants from osten-
> sive definitions that they give him; and he will often
> have to guess the meaning of these definitions; and
> will guess sometimes right, sometimes wrong.[2]

I have often had to guess in learning the language of
dependency. My method has been to offer my own words
and then wait for correction. Occasionally I have borrowed
descriptions from one person and tested them on another,
finding that people were intensely grateful to hear that
someone else had experienced the same feelings or come
to the same realizations under entirely different circumstances.

Words such as "waiting" and "boredom" eventually
began to acquire a special meaning for me. Activities such
as going to the bathroom or selecting items at the grocery
store began to assume significance. Observing and helping
people cope with their loss of autonomy, I gradually became conversant with their experiences. Yet my position
outside the world of illness and disability has, I hope, en-
abled me to describe its contours with the impartial eye of a
visitor.

Illness and disability alter our lives in basic ways. As

soon as our mobility becomes impaired, changes occur in how we spend our time and conduct our relationships. Having time on our hands soon becomes more of a burden than a privilege, and depending on others for help quickly becomes wearying. Self-esteem often erodes along with our physical capacities, and we may be further hurt by the degrading reactions that others have to our frailty. Regret for wasted time and unfulfilled dreams may nag at us, causing us to question the priorities around which we had previously organized our lives.

There are rich prospects for revival within these difficulties, but they require a reconstruction of our internal world. As we struggle with each downturn in an illness, our emotions become increasingly raw. Fixed aspects of our personality may begin to loosen. The courage to accede to such changes tends to arise slowly and fitfully. Eventually, our attitude toward our remaining years may transform, but not until we have revised our view of ourselves and our comprehension of the past.

My goal is to foster this process of revival at the same time that I render it intelligible to bystanders. Adult children taking care of aging parents, as well as relatives and friends assisting younger people with debilitating illnesses, will find that their capacity to be truly helpful enlarges with their understanding of these struggles. People in the predicament of dependency may recognize themselves in the stories quoted throughout the book, perhaps hastening their own renewal by gathering clues from what others have experienced.

Until recently, women took care of those who could not take care of themselves: the very young, the disabled, and the very old. Now that women have been liberated from the home along with men, no one may be at home to give care. Generally, the only people inside the houses of America during the day are the old and the sick, and they tend to be by themselves. A fifty-two-year-old woman told me about trying to keep her full-time job while caring for her disabled husband at home:

> He had a really bad stroke when he was forty-eight years old. Now he's fifty-five. It's been seven years. I don't know how I've done it. I have to wait until my supervisor goes to the restroom so I can call him and check up on him. Sometimes he leaves the burner on after lunch and I have to remind him to shut it off. I live in fear of the house burning down. For a while I had a supervisor who let me do my calls without sneaking, but the one I have now is awful. She acts like we're not supposed to have any other life but the work we do here. It's crazy, because I'd have my mind more on the work if I could get rid of my worry by making my calls.

The difficulties of old age may come sooner than we think. The increasing prevalence of AIDS, cancer, and other potentially incapacitating diseases calls upon all of us to prepare for the day when we may need other people's assistance with our daily survival or may need to render such help. The fastest growing population group in our country is people over the age of eighty-five, and the prevalence of disability in this group is fifty-eight percent.[3] The majority of people over the age of sixty-five are able to take care of themselves, but most live in fear of eventual frailty. Few of us will be exempt from the experience of illness, either through giving or receiving care, but we can strengthen our endurance by learning all that we can about the inner workings of dependency.

Acknowledgments

The major contributors to this undertaking were the people whose stories are quoted throughout the book. I have developed the themes of each chapter around their accounts, rather than starting with my own view and searching for verification. For this reason, the book has been a true exploration, and I owe my greatest thanks to my patients over the past ten years and to those whose published statements I have quoted.

I also want to thank my preliminary readers, those who took home early versions of the chapters and scribbled their reactions in the margins. Without them, I would not have been able to weed out confusing passages or find the nub of ideas that needed further development. My gratitude goes to Jana Ostrom, Donna Radcliffe, Barbara Bachtell, Rose St. Amand, Fred Lippert, Betsy Lieberman, Nikki Nichols, Christine Bagley, Joan Truskoff, Tom Heller, Alisa Malloch, Ed Ryan, Scott Glascock, Joyce McCollough, Victoria Toy-Gibbs, Joe Martin, Peter Londborg, Jill Bailey, Mark Fleming, Tom Watson, Kerry Harpster, Anne Danford, Julie Rush, Gloria Albetta, Sonja Cain, John Freeman, and Lauren Grosskopf.

Special appreciation is due to Gregg Zachary and Valerie Trueblood, professional writers who read and commented on the manuscript with considerable care. Their suggestions and encouragements were especially vital.

Energetic dialogue is also necessary to a writer. For this, I am grateful to the group at Ross Manor which met every Tuesday during the last year of the writing process. Our discussions were a consistent source of perspective, fresh ideas, and laughter.

Certain people participated in the book from the start, by helping me believe in the importance of the topic and in my capacity to see it through. For this, I am indebted to Patricia Richert, Marta Richardson, Marli Martin, Sue Tomita, Kathy Sullivan, Doug Noble, Stan Henry, Linda Hermans, Richard Goldman, David Barash, and my grandmother, Dorothy Bobrow.

Finally, I want to thank my husband, Barry Grosskopf. He read several versions of each chapter and never offered praise unless he felt the text deserved it. Many times I handed him a chapter and eagerly awaited his response, only to return to the manuscript an hour later, deflated. His characteristic frankness became as generative in the book as it is in our lives. Out of this repeated process of creation and revision, elation and dejection, a book emerged that I am pleased to offer to a wider public.

ONE

A Desert of Time

A woman who found herself confined by illness in her eighties writes:

> Age is a desert of time—hours, days, weeks, years per-haps—with little to do. So one has ample time to face everything one has had, been, done; gather them all in: the things that came from the outside, and those from inside. We have time at last to make them truly ours.[1]

The capacity to enjoy a homebound life may have more to do with our lifelong habits than our personality traits. Those who have always made the time to write, read, garden, make paintings, practice crafts, or play music reach their years of frailty with these routines firmly in place. So long as their ailments do not interfere with their skills, such people often thrive with time on their hands. The writer May Sarton writes, "Growing old is certainly easier for peo-ple like me who have no job from which to retire at a given age. I can't stop doing what I have always done, trying to sort out and shape experience."[2]

The rest of us face a difficult transition when our days become sedentary. We are forced into learning how to live with inactivity and how to keep ourselves engaged despite the absence of schedules and obligations. Kathleen Fischer,

1

a counselor and theologian, asserts, "In the later years we are asked to value *being* over *having*, but life has not trained us well for *being*."[3]

At any point in the lifespan, physical incapacity can compel us into "being" rather than "having," and into depending on others rather than doing for ourselves. We are then subjected to other people's timing, to what our helpers choose to give us and to the rhythms they impose. Time for "being" may become time for raging, to the extent that busy friends and relatives keep us waiting for hours on end. Additionally, our own body may thwart and disappoint us as we persist in trying to do things for ourselves. This chapter probes the process of adjusting to a captive dependence, examining the altered experience of time and relationships that ensues.

NOTHING TO DO

Working people yearn for days to do as they please. They relish the absence of commitments during weekends and vacations, believing that this ease awaits them when they retire. Leisure seems to hold the promise of unlimited pleasures and chosen involvements. They are usually unable to foresee the trial that free time actually becomes when there is no end to it and when options for filling it are circumscribed.

Ill and retired people have access to a paradoxical truth: it is easier to live with the mandatory activity of work or child-rearing than to create voluntary purposes every day. In the long run, days that are empty of obligation are exhausting. We have to push such days forward, while days that are full of commitments seem to move along by their own propulsion. A newly retired man describes his disappointment with the way he has used his first six months of open time:

> There has been no instant, miraculous opening of bright new paths. . . . Am I now squandering time because I have no real vital push to seize and exercise that freedom?[4]

This man lost his "vital push" once his leisure became boundless. He found that his experience of time slackened into lassitude. After the first few months of retirement, many people begin to struggle with getting out of bed in the morning. Unless a dog is waiting to be walked or someone is expecting them at a predetermined time, they find that the temptation to linger in bed becomes overwhelming.

It is humiliating to have little going on in one's life. Waiting for the mail and waiting for meals can take up the better part of a day, unless other involvements dwarf their importance. Sheepishly, this man goes on to admit that he makes "too much" of the mail:

> If I swivel halfway to the right I command the road down which the mailman comes, his lights flashing whenever he makes a stop. By frequent swiveling I can monitor his approach and be ready to pounce out the front door a split second after he begins to pull away. . . . I yield to the weak waste of time involved in waiting breathlessly for the mailman.[5]

In retirement homes everywhere, residents congregate in the lobby when the time for the mail draws near. Once a day, six days a week, the outside world intrudes upon an overly safe and predictable life. There is a rush of excitement for the possibility of being surprised. Prior to mealtimes, many wait outside the dining room more than an hour before the doors open. The mail and meals break up the blank expanse of the day into liveable segments: "after the mail comes," "before lunch."

In instituting the seven-day week and the Sabbath, the ancient Hebrews implemented an essential wisdom about time and motivation. The contrast between a day of rest and days of work adds an enlivening rhythm to life. Without clear distinctions, time runs together into an undifferentiated mass. A woman in a retirement home was asked by a fellow resident, "What do you do when you don't know what you want to do?"[6] The schedule was full of entertainments, but nothing in the program drew her. Going or not going to these activities was all the same.

In a book about the history and meaning of the seven-day week, Eviatar Zerubavel observed:

> The week disrupts the otherwise continuous flow of our everyday life on a regular basis and, in doing that, adds more dimensions to our existence. . . . [It] is a cycle of periodic alternation between opposites. . . . From an experiential standpoint, the most distinctive feature of this cycle is the fact that it helps to introduce discontinuity into our life.[7]

We thrive on discontinuity. We are stimulated by the "alternation between opposites" that work and pleasure offer us. If one day cannot be distinguished from the next by unusual occurrences, there are no markers upon which memory can anchor itself. Knowing whether it is Tuesday or Wednesday becomes a matter of checking what is printed on the daily newspaper rather than retrieving recognition from within. Such vagueness about the days of the week is often attributed to dementia rather than to this more common mental starvation.

To be starved for motion and exercise is yet another

depletion. Those for whom physical exertion was their chief form of release and renewal have to contend with a particularly onerous period of adjustment. A seventy-one-year-old man describes the torment he feels in being confined to home:

> Day after day, I have nothing to do. I have bad breathing and my legs are bad. . . . They hurt or they just won't go. I sit here, look out the window. The feelings are real, real deep in you, deep inside. It's bad on rainy days, especially; there's no hope of going out. . . . Can you imagine what it's like for a man who's been athletic all his life to be cut down in this way?[8]

When physical problems enclose us in a daily life in which everything has been mastered and repeated, the pull to keep returning to bed becomes more and more compelling. Life starts to echo the stasis of the body. One woman testifies to the power of this withering:

> I woke to my seventy-eighth birthday. And now my body dictated my days. Here was my house, my bedroom, my bed, my table full of books. Here was I, half propped up, large pillow under my knees, heating pad at my back. . . . Every couple of hours my body needed to move and I wandered around, to get something, replace something, realign something, water a plant or two. Then back to bed. Once in a while I strolled a little way outside, praying I would meet no one.[9]

We tend to shun the company of others when we feel we have nothing to say. With little going on in our lives beyond eating and sleeping, we fear that other people's contrasting vitality would shame us even as it momentarily revived us. When company leaves, we expect to be left emptier for having been so briefly filled. This woman found in the emptiness that her mind "worked like a disturbed hill of ants." Having nowhere to flee, she admits, "by day I waited for the night to come. At night I waited for the day."[10]

For homebound people, waiting becomes an absolute condition of daily living, rather than a fleeting effort. Week after week, they see nothing but the well-known walls of their homes and the glow of the television. Outings for them become a sensual circus, so pleasurable is it to see, hear, and smell the chaos of the outside world. When they are promised an afternoon out on the town, many count the hours until the time which is to be different from a hundred other afternoons. In his novel *The Magic Mountain*, Thomas Mann observes:

> When one day is like all the others, then they are all like one. . . . Habituation is a falling asleep or fatiguing of the sense of time; which explains why young years pass slowly, while later life flings itself faster and faster upon its course. We are aware that the intercalation of periods of change and novelty is the only means by which we can refresh our sense of time, strengthen, retard, and rejuvenate it, and therewith renew our perception of life itself. Such is the purpose of our changes of air and scene; . . . it is the secret of the healing power of change and incident.[11]

WAITING

The more dependent we are on the mercy of others, the more waiting we have to endure. Dependence and waiting eventually become synonymous. We cannot cancel arrangements to secure the necessities of life, and most of us do not have a fresh supply of helpers to replace those who keep us waiting beyond our endurance. One seventy-eight-year-old homebound woman described how she felt waiting for her daughter to take her grocery shopping:

> If she says she'll take me shopping sometime on Saturday, I get dressed early and go sit by the window. I like to be ready when she pulls into the driveway. I'm afraid to start on anything, because she could come any minute. If she doesn't come until two or three in the afternoon, I end up wasting a whole day waiting for her. I get mad at her, but I shouldn't. After all, she's doing me a favor. I have all day, and she's got to fit me into everything else in her life.

Waiting emphasizes the inferior status of the person who is being helped. This woman guards against keeping her daughter waiting on the driveway, recognizing the wide disparity between them: she needs her daughter in order to survive, but her daughter does not need her. She has "all day," while the daughter has to "fit" the errand into an array of doings. Her daughter's presence is in demand, while her presence is vital to no one. Each minute of waiting that accumulates speaks this inferiority more loudly.

These disparate conditions can evoke bitterness in the most loving of relationships. Anyone who has ever endured an incapacitating illness knows that the feelings evoked by days of waiting can be harder to bear than the illness itself. Emerson wrote:

> We wish to be self-sustained. We do not quite forgive a giver. The hand that feeds us is in some danger of being bitten. . . . We somehow hate the meat which we eat, because there seems something of degrading dependence in living by it.[12]

The freedom to come and go as we please, the "wish to be self-sustained," is as fundamental to most of us as breathing. When this part of our human endowment is frustrated, a subterranean anger is stirred. The truth of dependence is the urge to "bite" one's helpers, especially if no end to the dependence is in sight.

The longer an illness or incapacity lasts, the harder it becomes for us to maintain faith in our helpers' good will. We can see the constraints and the interferences that our needs necessarily impose on others. We begin to imagine the possibility of abandonment. Most of us believe that if we draw on our helpers' good will too often, we will use it up. We silently add up the sum of past favors, worrying how many more are left and having no way to measure the extent of this inner quantity.

Days of waiting can crack the confidence of the most secure people, given enough time and the wearing effects of doubt. In situations of dependence, we are asked to believe that we have accumulated vast stores of good will from our own acts of generosity in the past. In truth, most of us carry reservoirs of guilt from the many occasions when we failed to be as generous as we could have been. To then depend upon those whom we once disappointed opens up fears of retribution: "Will my son try to get back at me, now that I need him?"

We begin to scrutinize our helpers' faces for signs of reluctance. We usually derive little security from verbal assurances that our friends and relatives are happy to be of help. We have hours to ruminate over a moment's hesitation when we last asked someone for a ride, or to replay snippets of a conversation in which we overheard ourselves referred to as a "problem." We can dwell upon the memory of all discussion ceasing when we walked into a living room full of relatives, or worry about the day when we saw unmistakable signs of fatigue on a daughter's face.

We begin to wonder, "Is my life really worth all of this stress?" We see that every visit is for the accomplishment of a task and every phone call is to get an aspect of our survival organized. Ultimately, it can seem that our chief purpose left in life is to keep our caregivers from worrying about us and spending too much time on us. One homebound woman describes her efforts to conserve her requests for help:

> I read my paperbacks as slowly as I can. I ration out the chapters, because I don't want to finish them too quickly. Then, I start all over again with the first book. It works if I don't read too fast. I don't want to ask my daughter to give me a ride to the library or to make a special trip to a bookstore. She already does my shopping, cleans my house, and checks up on me every morning. It's too much already.

There are opposite responses to dependence, e.g., people who fold into the necessity of getting help with their daily lives as a relief from what had been an effortful independence. They welcome the collapse of the interpersonal boundaries which they had never really accepted. But most people resist dependence and struggle to maintain a secure sense of identity by asking for as little as they can.

One sixty-nine-year-old woman was so weakened by metastatic cancer that she could not avoid accepting help with cleaning her house, but she still held back from expressing the full extent of her needs:

> The doctor said I can't so much as pick up a vacuum cleaner, so my daughter helps me once a week. It kills

me to watch her. She doesn't like to bend under the kitchen table when she vacuums. She leaves the crumbs there, but I don't say anything. After she's gone, the crumbs drive me crazy. I stare at them all day. I can see them from where I sit in the living room. You can't imagine how they get to me, how I can't take my eyes off them. I say to myself, 'Next time, you'll tell her,' but I never do. She's doing so much for me already.

This woman was in mourning for herself. For over forty years in that house, she had vacuumed her breakfast crumbs every morning. If she had still been herself, the crumbs would have been gone. She stared at the crumbs day after day and saw her own demise.

Waiting for help is tied inexorably to waiting for death. Individuals have their own version of the crumbs, something that symbolizes who they used to be or how they used to live. The loss of this self is more threatening for many than the approach of their physical death. One woman with worsening arthritis was "resigned when she was no longer able to carry heavy objects or hold a paint brush, even though she loved her art classes. But when she realized that she could no longer make her own bed, she wept."[13] Healthy people often deride ill or frail people for what seems to be an over-focus on the trivial, not realizing the significance that can be contained in crumbs or an unmade bed.

TIME AND DISTANCE

The duress of frailty requires acceptance of its conditions, much as imprisonment mandates respect for simple freedoms. When Aleksandr Solzhenitsyn was being transferred

from one prison to another, he caught a glimpse of people
going about their lives:

> You have the right to arrange your own life under the
> blue sky and the hot sun, to get a drink of water, to
> stretch, to travel wherever you like. . . . Do not pursue
> what is illusory—property and position: all that is
> gained at the expense of your nerves decade after dec-
> ade, and is confiscated in one fell night. . . . It is
> enough if you don't freeze in the cold and if thirst and
> hunger don't claw at your insides. If your back isn't
> broken, if your feet can walk, if both arms can bend, if
> both eyes see and if both ears hear, then whom should
> you envy?[14]

Illness and imprisonment both teach that all can be
taken away "in one fell night." Prior to this kind of blow to
our pretensions, it is easy enough to live without looking
around, getting things done and not bothering to exert attention or appreciation. We reject aimlessness, even for an
hour. Everything we do has to serve the imperatives of our
future needs. In a hurried life, obliviousness comes down
around us like a curtain. There are only rare moments
when the curtain is pulled aside and we are graced with a
vivid sense of aliveness. Virginia Woolf called these inter-
ludes "moments of being." She was dismayed at how much
of life is lived in the haze of "non-being":

> A great part of every day is not lived consciously. One
> walks, eats, sees things, deals with what has to be done;
> the broken vacuum cleaner; ordering dinner; writing
> orders to Mabel; washing; cooking dinner; bookbind-
> ing. When it is a bad day the proportion of non-being
> is much larger.[15]

In their seventies and eighties, many people learn for
the first time in their lives to enjoy "moments of being." A

seventy-two-year-old man in poor health tells how he finally allows himself "the sight of the first pussy willow in spring, the chance encounter with a friend, the ever-changing beauty of nature, a glimpse of a happy child, a sand lot baseball game."[16]

The distance elongated by disability can be shortened only by surrender, by a giving in to the present in this way. Attention can no longer be focused elsewhere, because cracks in the sidewalk can spell devastation and rushing footsteps can mean a jolting loss of balance. Sinking into the time it takes for joints to stop aching or a heart to stop racing lets us enter into the spectacle around us. Shakespeare wrote, "Meantime, let wonder seem familiar."[17] Once we begin to make use of the "meantime," the interval between where we live and where we are going, we gradually become accustomed to immersing ourselves in wonder.

Many older people have to hang onto parking meters while they catch their breath or hunch over mailboxes until the aching in their legs subsides. They learn to measure distances in rest periods rather than yards. One woman explains: "I find I slowly exchange time for timing—pace, rhythm, tempo in the musical sense—and that includes rests."[18] The time needed for breathing and aching can be passed by watching the shapes of clouds blowing overhead. An eighty-year-old man wrote rapturously of his acquiring the ability to live in the corporeal present:

> . . . simply sitting still, like a snake on a sun-warmed stone, with a delicious feeling of indolence that was seldom attained in earlier years. A leaf flutters down, a cloud moves by inches across the horizon. At such moments the older person, completely relaxed, has become a part of nature—and a living part, with blood

coursing through his veins. The future does not exist
for him . . . now he has nothing more to win or lose.[19]

Frail people with walkers often can advance only three
or four inches at a time. Such slow headway challenges the
very notion of what it means to get somewhere. To the
healthy and able-bodied rushing by them, their progress
along the sidewalk can seem as senseless as it is laborious.
Why venture out under these conditions? The answer lies
in realms that are invisible to those who still retain control over their own progress in life. A man whose lung
condition made him breathless after just a few steps explained:

> I can't drive anymore and I can't get on the damn bus,
> but you're crazy if you think I'm gonna bug my daugh-
> ter each time I need a quart of milk. That's all there is
> to it. You go because you have to, because you want to
> be in charge of your own life.

Those who venture out despite frailty are accomplish-
ing more than attaining destinations. This man prefers his
precarious journey out on the streets to his helpless security
inside his apartment. It is less demeaning to wait for his
breath than to wait for his daughter's help. Walking con-
notes mastery over our lives, just as waiting for help conveys
a loss of mastery. A researcher who interviewed forty-seven
older men in an urban area found that "walking can be
viewed as a major metaphor . . . representing a continued
ability to live independently, to control events, and to be
active."[20]

Beyond the basic physical satisfactions, the components of life's sweetness are individual inventions. I once
asked a seventy-eight-year-old man tethered to an oxygen

tank due to severe emphysema how he lives with his situation:

> I like to get out. It makes me feel like I'm still alive. I
> look at the people going by, and they stare at my oxy-
> gen tank and the tubing in my nose. I start talking to
> them, to get conversations going. It's easy. People like
> to talk. They'll tell you anything. I get their whole life
> story sometimes. It's really interesting. Otherwise, I'd
> be sitting in the lobby staring straight ahead like all
> those other people in my building. They look like they
> died ten years ago. I'd start looking like them if I stayed
> in there.

This man had always found delight in the human spectacle,
and this delight now drives him out onto the streets despite
his breathlessness.

When it takes a half hour to walk a city block, distances
have to be calculated with the skill of a physicist and the
courage of an adventurer. Velocity is determined by short-
ness of breath, a racing heart, aching knees, or the constraints of fear. At what distance will a bench become vital?
Quivering legs could mean a fall, and a fall could lead to a
nursing home. Getting from here to there and back again is
no longer as simple as completing a linear sequence.

If resisted, both time and distance can become subject
to a maddening elongation. Instead, throughout the life-
span, Thoreau advocates the practice of simple savoring:

> Health requires this relaxation, this aimless life. This
> life in the present. . . . I keep out of doors for the sake
> of the mineral, vegetable, and animal in me. . . . What
> are threescore years and ten hurriedly and coarsely
> lived to moments of divine leisure in which your life is
> coincident with the life of the universe? We live too

fast and coarsely, just as we eat too fast and do not know the true savor of our food.[21]

People who are able to live well in spite of illness are those who allow "divine leisure" to crowd their physical hardships out of center stage.

§

Turning the "nothing" of empty time into the "something" of good days is the alchemy of successful frailty. At first, having too much time on our hands can feel like a daily humiliation in our making so little of it. Waiting for help emphasizes all the dignities and freedoms that have been ripped away from us. Gradually, if we do not become hardened in our disappointment, we can turn the insults of illness into privileges of being. A man who had a heart attack in his fifties writes:

> Afterward, day by day I learned as if for the first time what living is. During the first days after the heart attack, I felt distant from those who worked upon me and from those who visited me in the intensive care unit. I was aware of their healthily beating hearts, but with envy and with loneliness. . . . As the days went on, I began to perceive the healthy people around me with more and more joy. Now when I walk down the street and see a child who is lithe as a cat, or an adult who is strolling with the unself-conscious poise of health, I rejoice with them.[22]

T W O _____

The Quality of Mercy

Aristotle believed that the search for virtue is necessarily circular:

> Not everyone can find the middle of a circle, but only a man who has the proper knowledge. Similarly, anyone can get angry—that is easy—or can give away money or spend it; but to do all this to the right person, to the right extent, at the right time, for the right reason, and in the right way is no longer something easy that anyone can do. It is for this reason that good conduct is rare, praiseworthy, and noble.[1]

Helping "to the right extent, at the right time, for the right reason, and in the right way" has never been something easy. What is truly merciful changes from day to day, even from hour to hour. Often, we have to go to the extremes of doing too much or too little for someone before we can find the "right extent" of helping.

The word mercy has fallen out of common usage in our language. It derives from the Old French *merci,* which meant compassion and forbearance toward someone in one's power. In Latin, *merces* signifies pay or reward, and the root *merc* refers to aspects of commerce.[2] The words merchant and mercenary at first seem antithetical to mercy, and one wonders at their common root. But when we have to give help or depend on others for help, we understand why the concept of exchange underlies both usages.

Mercy is based entirely on exchange. Giving help eventually embitters us, unless we are compensated at least by appreciation; accepting help degrades us, unless we are convinced that our helpers are getting something in return. As much as we might prefer to reject this stark accounting, we discover in living through situations of dependence that good will is not enough. This chapter probes the delicate balance at the heart of mercy, showing how reciprocation replenishes both the spirit of the helper and the person who is helped.

NECESSARY POWERS

Those who depend on others for daily survival often feel their very existence is an imposition. Nancy Mairs, a forty-three-year-old writer with multiple sclerosis, describes "a relentless pressure to please—to prove myself worth the burdens I impose."[3] Many ill people suppress complaints and avoid asserting themselves, believing that they owe every possible accommodation to those who help them survive. This sense of indebtedness is renewed day after day, with each cuff someone fastens for them and each errand run on their behalf.

I once counselled a man whose stroke had deprived him of the ability to speak and write. I found him immobilized at his kitchen table, barely responsive to my presence. I tried to ask him questions that could be answered with a shake of the head, but his wife kept interrupting. She said

that he could not go off driving anymore by himself, because it was too dangerous. He could not walk over to the
grocery store a few blocks away, because he was unable to
ask for anything. She went on and on, and her husband
stared straight ahead, his face completely frozen. Finally, I
looked into his eyes. There was fire in them. I said, "You're
angry." He nodded and started hitting the back pocket of
his pants with his hand and pointing at his wife. He slapped
harder and harder. I struggled to figure out what he was trying to say. Then I understood. "Your wallet. Where is your
wallet?" I asked. He pointed more vigorously at his wife,
"Oh," she said, "I'm storing it in his desk. He doesn't need
it any more."

After his wallet was returned, this man began to walk
around his neighborhood and to smile triumphantly at his
wife. Carrying written notes to the grocer, he started buying
milk and bread at the local store. Gradually, he became less
depressed and began working with the speech therapist on
using other communication devices. Repossessing his wallet allowed this man to feel like himself again and to reach
into the outside world, in spite of his speechlessness.

Taking care of a person does not have to entail having
power over major aspects of his or her life, but frailty seems
to invite invasion. The need to get things done is so press-
ing and time limitations are so severe that it soon becomes
simpler to omit the person's participation in small decisions and routines. Survival easily comes to seem more
compelling than dignity. A sixty-two-year-old woman who
was paralyzed on one side by a stroke told me about her
feelings:

> You can't imagine how helpless I feel. Take my kitchen
> sink. A sink isn't clean unless you scrub it first with
> cleanser and then disinfectant. At least that's the way

I've always done it. I can't even reach my sink now. The chore worker swishes around some suds and says it's done and I want to jump out of the wheelchair and do it myself. But I'm trapped in this chair, in this body, and I'm supposed to be glad that I have help. But I'm not glad. I'm furious.

So long as we still possess it, the power to carry out simple intentions is one of the many unnoticed pleasures of life. When we lose it, we see what it means to do the most ordinary things our own way. This woman's sink is only one of the areas in which she can no longer exert influence or get things done in accordance with her wishes. When others have to serve as our arms and hands, asking that a sink be cleaned exactly as we would have done it seems absurd. Anything but a "thank you" for the help seems ungrateful. Lest we be regarded as a burden, most of us rage inwardly about the complaints we are afraid to voice and the desires we dare not impose.

Some people make rebellious bids for control that they then keep secret from their helpers. One sixty-two-year-old woman recounted her acts of defiance to me, on the condition that I not repeat them to her daughter:

I had a fall down the basement steps, and so my daughter says she'll throttle me if I ever go down there. She hired a woman to come in and do my wash once a week so I never have to go down there. But I do go down. My daughter doesn't know it and I'm very careful, but once in a while I get the crazy urge to do whatever I want to do. It's as simple as that. It's my house, my basement, my washing machine, and my life. That's the way I feel.

Submission does not come easily to people who have spent decades running their own lives. Going down those steps made this woman's basement her own again, just as choosing to violate her daughter's restriction made her life her own again. Seizing freedom can be as unreasonable as it is gratifying.

Those who have had their wings clipped by illness or old age often feel the need to do something "crazy" to remind themselves that they are still able to exert influence, if only over their own domain or their own body. This need conflicts with their feeling obliged to give full cooperation to their caregivers. When other means of repayment are lacking, compliance does become the only resource that can be exchanged for sustenance. James Dowd, a sociologist, affirms this:

> [Power] is derived from imbalances in the social exchange. . . . The relative power of the aged vis-à-vis their social environment is gradually diminished until all that remains of their power resources is the humble capacity to comply. . . . [For instance,] the widowed woman living with her married children may be required to exchange compliance or approval for her room and board.[4]

Those with personality styles that prevent their squelching themselves in this manner lack even the power of compliance. Instead, they turn their helplessness into its reverse, commanding their helpers to follow their exact specifications and blasting their helpers with anger when their directives are not heeded. Not surprisingly, such people are dreaded by hired workers and family helpers alike. Their company is shunned, except when the performance of duties necessitates interaction. They become more and more isolated emotionally as their sullen helpers get the work done but infuse little warmth into their labors.

For those receiving care but craving control, the

"right" amount of self-assertion is always complicated. Personality and life history must be taken into consideration. For instance, if a wife is providing care to her ill husband, useful compromises in their marriage may have been disrupted by the illness. Years may have passed since they last negotiated their power balance or had to make adjustments for each other's personality style.

A seventy-six-year-old man whose hand tremor interfered with his writing checks explained the process of disruption and renegotiation that took place in his fifty-five year marriage:

> Watching my wife ruin the checkbook was driving me crazy. She would just dash off the bills, not bothering to mark down the dates, check numbers, who it was to, all that stuff. A couple of times she didn't even mark down the amount. How the hell could I balance the checkbook without the amounts? It was making me sick. Finally, we made a deal—that I could stand over her head to make sure she did it right, so long as I stayed out of her hair in the kitchen. That was fair.

This man needed control over the household finances more than he needed a say in meal preparation. His wife needed at least one arena in which she was not subject to her husband's meticulous instruction and criticism. Their trade was based on recognition of what was most important to each, not merely on pragmatic considerations. In situations of dependence, it is easy to get lost in the pressures of the practical and to put aside preferences that are not strictly "necessary."

Every detail of checkbooks and kitchens cannot be negotiated, and not all preferences can be respected. The trick for caregivers and dependent people is to find small but specific concessions to each other's preferences that yield large satisfactions. There is no formula for this process beyond the most basic concept of exchange, such as "You do this for me and I'll do that for you." Such exchanges tend to multiply feelings of efficacy, even as they divide actual opportunities for wielding power.

In my clinical practice, I have found that most family members giving care to an ill relative refuse even to mention the word "power," as if power and affection cannot coexist. When their disempowered relative becomes depressed, they mistake this despondency for an accusation that they are not doing a good job. Hoping for appreciation, they instead get quietly hostile acquiescence. Once families acknowledge the presence and importance of power in situations of dependency, they tend to have little difficulty taking stock of its distribution and beginning to remedy imbalances on either side. The next section explores what happens when caregivers give up too much power by sacrificing their needs and suppressing their complaints.

THE PREVENTION OF RESENTMENT

Resentment is a reliable gauge of when helpers are doing more than they should. The problem with heeding this gauge is that there are ongoing pressures to deny its validity. Dedicated helpers insist that they are doing "fine." At all costs, they want to avoid evoking the ill person's fear of abandonment and to keep from revealing that the care has become burdensome. They conceal their feelings and strive to maintain a contented exterior. Eventually, their pretense isolates them from the ill person, and any previous intimacy becomes veiled by this effort to hide the truth.

Warning others against such pretending, an adult

daughter wrote an article called "The Sandwich Generation." She felt herself sandwiched between her husband,
her children, her job, and her mother's need for frequent
contact with her. Each time she visited her mother, she
feigned an attitude of successful coping, while inside she
felt tense and overwhelmed. Finally, she came to a crucial
realization: "I began to see how my mother's illness had become a wall between us." She went on:

> The next time we were together I held her hands very
> tight in mine, as if to pass my strength to her, and told
> her that I couldn't bear the distance between us. If the
> time that remained to us was to have any meaning at
> all, I said, we would have to speak of our feelings. . . .
> And so we began to talk. We agreed on a schedule of
> visits and phone calls that made my life less chaotic
> and gave me more time and energy for my own family.
> But more important, as we began to speak honestly the
> wall between us started to break down. "I feel guilty
> because I'm taking you away from your children," she
> confessed. And I told her, "I wish I could care for you
> better," admitting how hard it was for me to be mother
> to my mother.[5]

Unacknowledged weariness puts a barrier between ill
people and those who assist them. But feelings leak through
in subtle ways. A strained voice or tension in the grip of a
hand are difficult to conceal. Ill people who fear becoming
a burden stay alert for just such nuances. This woman's
mother felt guilty all along because she had been aware of
her daughter's stress and dividedness. For both mother and
daughter, admitting the truth was not nearly so agonizing as
avoiding it had been.

Ill people often grapple with painful ambivalence

about continuing to accept help that they know is burdening members of their family. At the same time that they wish to release their loved ones, they want to cling to the comfort they provide. One seventy-five-year-old woman told me how she lay awake at night for months, ruminating over whether to free her son from his imprisoning helpfulness:

> My son says he likes fixing me dinner every night, but he looks so tense when he's here. He comes over right from work, and his wife holds dinner at their house until he gets home. He smiles, makes chitchat, but I know he's racing against time. Sometimes he looks like he's going to explode, his face is so tight, but he keeps on smiling. I wish he could just say it's too much for him. I'd be disappointed, don't get me wrong, but TV dinners wouldn't kill me.

This woman saw that beneath his cheerful demeanor her son was suffering, but she did not initiate his release from the obligation. She was afraid, not of TV dinners but of the loneliness that would await her on a nightly basis if she spoke up and urged him to visit her only on weekends. The worst consequence of her silence was the gap it left between them. He could no longer speak with her beyond the level of "chitchat" because she herself had become the unmentionable problem in his life. Ironically, her loneliness would perhaps have lessened if she had exchanged frequent contact with him on weekdays for more relaxed contact on weekends.

Here again is the notion of exchange: trading frequency for quality, guilty silence for relieving honesty. Dependent people and their helpers can release each other from guilt, but gestures must be mutual if they are to be effective. I met one daughter who had instinctively begun a series of positive exchanges with her ill mother, thus discovering the quality of mercy on her own:

> My mother was on oxygen and bedbound. Taking care of her twenty-four hours a day was wiping me out. I kept waiting on her hand and foot, getting her whatever she wanted whenever she wanted it. One day I heard her calling me from upstairs and I actually hated her voice. I went cold all over. Then I knew it was time to stop this perfect daughter stuff. Who wants to be hated? I wasn't doing her any favors. So I started spending a few hours a day outside in my garden, just leaving her a pitcher of water beside her bed. She had to wait to go to the bathroom sometimes, but so what. It was worth it to her. I started liking her again, doing sweet things for her. She looked so much happier when I stopped being so perfect. I wish I had realized sooner that this was more important.

The reward for recognizing resentment as a limit is enjoying the ill person's company again. To feel that one can give pleasure and to receive small acts of sweetness is a fair exchange for a few hours' wait. A spiral of good feeling was set in motion between this mother and daughter, replacing the negative spiral that had been evolving between them as the daughter was becoming more and more weary of the care. If given the choice, few people would choose being waited on over being enjoyed.

Unfortunately, instigating enjoyment is often difficult when life has become constricted by illness, bereavement, or the sheer tedium of subsistence. Within this limited range, aging parents and adult children are often reduced to holding onto opposite ends of an obligation. They come to feel that little binds them together except abject duty. One daughter came to me because she was unable to get resentment out of her voice when her father made his nightly calls to her. In the four years since her mother's death, her adoring relationship with her father had turned sour. He was almost continually despondent, and she had grown impatient trying to cheer or comfort him. She expressed her dilemma clearly:

> I hear my father's voice on the phone and my heart sinks. It's awful to feel this way, but I know he's going to tell me how lonely he is and how much he misses Mom. I'm sick of hearing about it. I've heard it so many times already and there's nothing I can do about it. The worst part of it is he always calls just as my husband and I are lying down in bed together. This is the time of night when he misses Mom the most, but it's also our time, our time to be together, and I resent my father terribly then.

Saying these forbidden words, that she was "sick" of her father's loneliness, made her cry. Underneath this exasperation was her sadness that night after night of phone calls had made little impact on her father's sorrow. The crux of this session came when she suddenly saw that no amount of conversation was going to diminish her father's yearning for her mother's company, especially at that time of the night. She also realized that preserving the sanctity of her bedtimes with her husband celebrated what she had learned from her parents about making a marriage work. She made up her mind to tell him the truth.

A few weeks later, she announced that her father had reacted "wonderfully" to her honesty. Caught up in his sorrow, he had not noticed the poor timing of his calls, and he thanked her for stopping his intrusions into such a precious part of her day. Together they devised other ways he could cope with his worst moments, such as listening to a tape she made for him of childhood memories. This gave him both the sound of a familiar voice and a distraction back to happier times. She began to call him earlier in the evening, when it was most convenient for her. Almost immediately, she found that her resentment receded: "He's my father again, not just a weight on my back."

With frankness, ill people and those who assist them can begin to surmount the impasse created by unacknowledged power and unspoken resentment. Honesty also sets the stage for further, equally crucial corrections in the balance of the relationship.

TO BE OF USE

In a passage about his volunteer work as a visitor to homebound elderly, a seventy-seven-year-old man describes what happens each time he fails to find something that his clients can give him in return:

> The old person being visited knows that he is simply being visited. He knows that he is in receipt of a charitable act and that there is no true relationship. He knows that you and he have nothing in the world in common except old age. The old person knows that all too well, ah, too well.[6]

He goes on to tell the story of discovering a common passion for genealogy with one of his clients: "So we welcomed each other's craziness and became real friends at once." Suddenly the homebound man was not receiving charity but rather was participating in a pleasure. He was not "simply being visited," but rather was granting his visitor a chance to indulge and amplify his own interests.

The Roman historian Tacitus warned against generosity that cannot be returned. He stated that "services are welcome as long as it seems possible to repay them, but when they greatly exceed that point they produce not gratitude but hatred."[7] Frail people are generally denied chances to give something back to their helpers or to their communities. Their offers are refused with statements like, "You don't have to do that. We'll take care of everything." Helpers mean well, without realizing how urgently people in their care crave a tangible counterbalance to their dependency.

Americans tend to ignore the weight of shame and indebtedness that is carried long after someone receives assistance. Conversely, in Japanese culture owing gratitude to a benefactor is acknowledged as a hardship. The anthropologist Ruth Benedict notes that Japanese people "do not like to shoulder casually the debt of gratitude" and that this reluctance is reflected in the words they use to express indebtedness. She writes:

> The Japanese have many ways of saying "Thank you". . . . The least ambivalent, the phrase that has been adopted in modern city department stores, means "Oh, this difficult thing" (*arigato*). The Japanese usually say that this "difficult thing" is the great and rare benefit the customer is bestowing on the store in buying. . . . Other just as common words for "thank you" refer like *kino doku* to the difficulty of receiving. Shopkeepers who run their own shops most commonly say literally: "Oh, this doesn't end," (*sumimasen*), i.e., "I have received (an obligation) from you and under modern economic arrangements I can never repay you; I am sorry to be placed in such a position". . . . Another word for thank-you, *katajikenai*, which is written with the character "insult," "loss of face" . . . means both "I am insulted" and "I am grateful."[8]

When culture and language fail to acknowledge the difficulty of receiving, the dependent person is left doubly burdened, in disliking the help that cannot be repaid and in feeling guilty about the dislike. A forty-eight-year-old man with metastatic cancer explained what it is like to receive too much mercy:

> Ever since I got sick, everyone's been bringing me things—new blankets, special treats, even a new couch. I'm grateful for all this, but it gets to me. I mean, when Christmas came I got more fruit and candy than I could possibly eat. I went door-to-door here in my building and left little packages outside everybody's door. Now, that felt good. I was on the giving end for a change. That's what's missing in my life. I wish I had more I could give to people. Saying "thank you" all the time makes you feel bad.

Being of use makes being in need easier. This man "felt good" delivering his packages, imagining all the while the delighted surprise on his neighbors' faces when they opened their doors. As the French philosopher Montaigne wrote, "There is a sort of gratification in doing good which makes us rejoice in ourselves . . . and this natural rejoicing is a great boon to us, and the only payment that never fails us."[9]

As soon as opportunities to be useful become scarce, such as during times of illness, we appreciate the full meaning of Montaigne's remark. We wake up to the stark fact that no one expects our presence and no one needs our efforts. Lacking external obligations, we discover that we have to summon all of our resolve just to take care of bodily concerns. I have often heard people in these circumstances say, "Look at my life—all I do is eat and sleep. What kind of life is this?" They equate their lack of productive activity with worthlessness. One gerontologist writes, "With older people there often comes a point of having few responsibilities for others. At the same time a good and proper caring for self may lose importance."[10]

Mere existence does not imbue us with the will to thrive. An eighty-two-year-old woman once let me know her secret for enduring the pain of a degenerative spinal disease:

> I have a neighbor who can't see to take her pills. It's hard for me to get down the hall to her apartment, but she has to have the help. I wake up and I know I have to get down there, no matter what. My back hurts, but I have two good eyes. Thinking how she can't see takes my mind off my aching back. What would she do without me?

This woman does not have to rely upon her own fickle willpower each morning, but rather the necessity of meeting her neighbor's need for help. Every day she swings her legs over the side of her bed and gets dressed, in spite of the aching. She works hard to maintain her ability to walk that crucial distance down the hall. Three times a day, her neighbor's need ensures that she keeps her legs strong and her spirit supple. Obligations curtail our freedom to waste ourselves.

James Wallace, a philosopher of ethics, points out that people who are kind, generous, and compassionate give others "a striking affirmation of the intrinsic worth and importance of individual human beings."[11] But their good deeds and thoughts confirm the value of their lives for themselves as well. This insight was given ample demonstration by Barbara Myerhoff, an anthropologist, in her study of Jewish older people in an urban ghetto. She was struck by the vibrance of many of the women she interviewed, attributing their animation to their engagement in networks of giving and receiving help:

> The old women I have described communicated a quiet conviction and satisfaction with themselves ... in domestic religion, in caring for others, in serious, dedicated friendships, in constructing individual careers made of personally discovered projects, in arranging lives of self-care and attentiveness to others who are needy. . . .[12]

In spite of their own bereavements and infirmities, these women sought out the opportunity to perform acts of service. These commitments gave them reasons to transcend their own problems. Looking back on her research, Myerhoff comments, "Theirs is not a world in which something is given for nothing. Everything is built around exchange. There are no beggars, no charity, only webs of donors."[13] Through these "webs," dignity is passed around from one person to another and no one is left without the pride of being a donor.

To be of help to others is one of the highest honors in Jewish tradition, but the recipient of a *mitzvah,* a good deed, must not be shamed. In his portrait of Judaism's tenets, the philosopher Leon Roth explains, "The Rabbis of the Talmud held that to help one's fellow man is the best of all deeds but to bring shame on him is one of the worst: a man should be (like Job) 'eyes to the blind' without being himself seen."[14] In retirement homes and other communal settings, shame is a recurring obstacle to the formation of helping networks. What people encounter is a virtual conspiracy of independence.

The unwritten code in most of these settings is that residents are supposed to fend for themselves. The able-bodied shun those who appear to be frail, and frail people try to conceal their needs as much as they can. Writing about life in a retirement home, an eighty-five-year-old woman depicts her experience with this code in the cafeteria:

> Sometime, somewhere, the idea developed that one must neither give nor receive help in carrying the cafeteria trays. Occasionally, if someone has had an eye or a hand operation, the custom is varied for a short time, but soon those people are struggling with their trays again.[15]

Dreading pity more than hunger, many omit items from their trays in order to carry them without assistance. The resident quoted above continues: "We keep up with one another on the way to the elevator and in the hall . . . but we never visit inside our apartments."[16] Inside their residences are their badges of vulnerability: crumbs that cannot be vacuumed from the floor and unmade beds that fumbling hands can no longer correct. To visit each others' apartments would expose their frailties. Instead, they live in private cells, concealing the evidence of their incapacities and averting their eyes from each others' problems.

As a social worker, I have been admitted to many such apartments over the years. Usually, my presence was accepted only because a sudden illness had necessitated my help. In one such instance, I found that my client had been sitting in the dark for weeks. The light bulbs had burned out in her ceiling fixtures, and she had no floor or table lamps. Rather than ask one of her neighbors to help, she had been reading by daylight and going to bed when it became too dark to see. She explained:

> What can I do for my neighbors? Nothing. Look at my hands. They're useless from this arthritis. I can't keep asking for favors, day in and day out. They'll get sick of me. Pretty soon they'll see me coming and they'll duck

into their apartments. No, I'd rather do for myself or just do without.

This woman saw herself as a black hole of needs that other people should avoid, since she had "nothing" to give in return. At first, she flatly refused to let me stand on a stool and replace her bulbs. I insisted that it would make me happy to do this for her, and that I would take away with me the image of her reading again through the long winter night. She studied my face as I told her how I hated the idea of her tossing fitfully in bed, unable to sleep and unable to read. Finally, her pride relented and she led me to her supply of light bulbs. As I left, I thanked her for giving me the honor of helping her. She understood what I meant, for it was she who was carrying the burden of uselessness and I who was being granted satisfaction.

§

The one who gives help is more powerful than the one who receives it. The sheer acknowledgement of this inequality is a relief to those who have to occupy the inferior position. They no longer have to pretend that they are pleased, and they can insist upon forms of repayment other than compliance. Those who provide mercy can then accept consideration for their own needs without feeling guilty, and helping arrangements can be structured toward the aim of achieving a balanced exchange.

The highest qualities of mercy may not be fully achievable, but such efforts at least minimize degradation and relieve resentment. In his *Essays in Pragmatism,* William James affirms the complexity of striving for ethical ideals within the murky conditions of actual life:

The actually possible in this world is vastly narrower than all that is demanded; and there is always a *pinch* between the ideal and the actual which can only be got through by leaving part of the ideal behind. . . . Some part of the ideal must be butchered.[17]

Knowing what to do for an ill person and what to cease doing begins with understanding what life is like from that person's perspective. Without this comprehension, there is a tendency to worry about the wrong things and to give assistance in the wrong ways. Learning all that we can about being dependent allows us to fall short of the ideal to the right extent.

Bodily Terms

A man who spent several weeks confined to a hospital bed recalls what he learned:

> I was seriously ill and wasn't allowed to get out of bed
> or move at all, even if it was only to go from lying on
> one side to lying on the other. It was in that state of
> extreme helplessness that I saw how much a person
> can be in need of others. I was in need not only of the
> director of the medical staff and his interns and of the
> nurses, day and night, but also of the nurses' aides, the
> masseuse, and the orderlies. Not only for medical care,
> but for a comforting word or gesture.[1]

We are never the same after being reduced to bodily
terms. For the rest of our lives, we are unable to forget how
much it is possible to be in need of others. We approach our
relationships differently from then on, emphasizing those
bonds which seem likely to withstand the tests of time and
strain, and putting less effort into bonds of convenience.

The nature of our aspirations changes along with the
style of our relationships. We start asking different things
of life. In an essay, "On Being Ill," Virginia Woolf writes,
"Considering how common illness is, how tremendous the
spiritual change it brings, . . . it becomes strange indeed

that illness has not taken its place with love and battle and jealousy among the prime themes of literature."[2]

As a result of these changes, ill people can tell in a glance whether someone they meet has ever had the experience of being helpless. They notice that a gap separates them from those who continue to be beguiled by good health. They watch as friends and relatives go on living from day to day as if they are invincible, dwelling inside a privileged deception.

This chapter attempts to reduce this separation between the sick and the well. Healthy people often find themselves distracted by the crude exterior of illness, bypassing much of the complexity going on beneath the surface. Knowing what to say and do in the presence of a person who is incapacitated requires an awareness of what it is like to have time on one's hands and to be at the mercy of others, but also knowledge of the range of emotions that arise in reaction to helplessness itself.

GRATITUDE OR BITTERNESS

There is no middle ground in the stark appraisal of suffering. In *The Illness Narratives,* Arthur Kleinman notes, "The problem of illness as suffering raises two fundamental questions . . . Why me? (the question of bafflement), and What can be done? (the question of order and control)."[3] Our responses to these questions determine the course of our endurance.

Initially, most of us answer the question "Why me?" with anger, and the question "What can be done?" with despair. We oppose the lessons of helplessness, hardening ourselves against the indignities and rejecting the forced revision of our priorities. We hope only for recovery and for a return to self-sufficiency. Anything less invokes bitterness.

A man contending with the later stages of a severely disabling disease explains:

> First, you blame the illness. You say, "If only I wasn't so sick, life would be better for me." Then you blame other people, saying, "Life would be better if people didn't treat me like a cripple." Then, you finally realize it's what you put out there that determines how your life is and how people treat you. You *make* your life good—it doesn't just happen.[4]

There are countless pitfalls on the way out of misery. Focusing relentlessly on what has been lost, comparing oneself to others, aspiring for things that are out of reach, and placing blame on others are only some of the most common snares. Each personal variation is uniquely painful.

Fear comes in several permutations. A woman coping with breast cancer writes, "Sometimes fear stalks me like another malignancy, sapping energy and power and attention from my work."[5] A woman who lost all of her body hair as the first sign of an obscure and incurable illness enumerates the kinds of dread that illness evokes:

> We are afraid of the process of our illness, we are afraid of increasing loss of control, we are afraid of the outcome, and we are afraid of dying. . . . We are afraid of how [our families and friends] see us, how they feel about us, and how our condition affects their lives.[6]

Rage at all that is being taken away can also impede the surmounting of misery. Watching others adapt to our decline and seeing how our importance in their lives diminishes can sting beyond our capacity for grace. A woman who faced Lou Gehrig's disease in her early forties wrote in her journal: "This is like experiencing one's old age prematurely. [My husband] tells me how much everyone loves me, and sometimes I feel it. But their lives can go on so well without me."[7]

It can seem that there is no context in which the uglier emotions can be released. Resentment toward those who have taken our place and jealousy toward all who still possess their good health are reactions everyone sustains but few express. When we conceal these feelings, we end up choking inwardly as others praise our sham endurance. At the same time, those assisting us may be locked into a parallel isolation, shamed by feelings they dare not confess. A woman watching her husband slowly deteriorate from a heart condition writes about the feelings she tries to conceal:

> I ache for him, but I resent him as well, this sick, sunken man who is my beautiful Hal whom I adore. The intensity of the anger than hovers there, beneath what I take to be love, is frightening. I understand the wretched banality of such an anger as this, I do not have to be a professor of whatever to understand the how and the why of such an anger, yet it shames and appalls me. And of course, he knows.[8]

This isolation is worsened still further when friends keep their distance. In the economy of illness, the supply of friends tends to shrink. Peripheral friends drop away, since such relationships are reliant on contexts in which little effort has to be exerted. The wife of a man with Parkinson's disease states, "Friends, they don't *come* here very often. They phone me and tell me this and tell me that. But they don't actually *visit* here any more. They don't know how to behave towards him, I suppose."[9]

Once fear, rage, and isolation take hold of us, they can distract us from the solaces that may have helped us abide. It is easy to lose heart for coping. A woman describes the day she became overwhelmed by her husband's multiple sclerosis:

> I came home from work and found him lying on the floor. He'd been there all afternoon. I got a sheet and pulled him into the bedroom and somehow got him onto the bed. Then I went into another room and cried. That was it. I didn't see how we could go on. For days, I had no spirit for anything, like my heart had dropped out of me. Finally, I went to see our minister. He listened to me for a long time, and then he said, "I know so many widows—at least your husband is not dying." I was stunned. All I saw was the MS, not that I was lucky to still have my husband. I went home not too consoled. But a few days later, I started noticing how much companionship we still enjoyed, despite the condition of his body. It was all different after that, like a light had been turned on. We had twenty more good years together, and I never got so low again.

The word courage comes from the Latin *cor* for heart. We give ourselves fresh heart by pulling our attention away from what has been lost. It is not that fear and disheartenment can be willed away, but that we have to turn our focus in a direction most favorable to their alleviation. A woman who lived with muscular dystrophy for more than seventy years became a master of adapting to the successive losses exacted by her illness:

> Gradually, I developed my own philosophy for climb-ing out of the pit. Gloom is boredom, I would tell my-

self over and over again. To escape, I sought some new interest within my remaining abilities. One time I even took voice lessons. It was one of my darkest periods and, although I am not particularly musical and no one ever told me I could sing, I found a private teacher who would work with me.[10]

Mustering the courage to usurp gloom is not a once-and-for-all attainment. No sooner do we become accustomed to one set of conditions than illness imposes others. We have to keep devising satisfactions and then releasing our hold on them. Swinging from gratitude to bitterness and back again, the cycle moves with a fierce complexity. We either acquire enough flexibility to open ourselves to new consolations, or bitterness prevails.

The route to resilience begins with old strengths. A poet afflicted with a severe case of shingles, "one of the most painful and nerve-racking of illnesses," found a way to make his illness less grueling. He writes:

> I decided that instead of passively enduring the sleepless nights and difficult days, I must somehow rally and turn negative energy into positive. Consequently, I fell back upon my greatest strength and forced myself to write a poem almost every day in the late afternoon. Miraculously, the psychological release had a beneficial effect, and I could sleep from then on with little or no medication almost every night. Moreover, I wrote some of my best work as compensation for my illness.[11]

It is as if our habits have more force in their familiarity than do the alien incursions of sickness. We are carried by patterns back to ourselves. A woman who was too weak to carry a portable oxygen tank obtained a cord long enough to reach from her main tank into her garden. While pulling weeds and planting flowers, she told me, "My hands know what to do out here, and the rest of me goes right along with them. Out here, smelling the soil, I can breathe again. Better than with the pills."

In *Anatomy of an Illness*, Norman Cousins describes visiting with Pablo Casals shortly before the master cellist turned ninety. Casals' ritual each morning was to play piano:

> He arranged himself with some difficulty on the piano bench, then with discernable effort raised his swollen and clenched fingers above the keyboard. . . . The fingers slowly unlocked and reached toward the keys like the buds of a plant toward the sunlight. His back straightened. He seemed to breathe more freely. . . . He hummed as he played, then said that Bach spoke to him here—and placed his hand over his heart. Then he plunged into a Brahms concerto and his fingers, now agile and powerful, raced across the keyboard with dazzling speed. His entire body seemed fused with the music; it was no longer stiff and shrunken but supple and graceful and completely freed of its arthritic coils.[12]

Living requires courage under all circumstances, but especially when illness presides. We have to exert a deliberate effort, day by day, to make life as good as the body allows. Our will to live a circumscribed life arises directly from our realizing the value of each ability we have retained and each new capacity we have acquired. It is like maintaining neatness in a household that is always verging on disorder: there can be no slackening of attention, or discouragement rushes in.

After her stroke, the writer May Sarton found herself in a state of abject decline, "cut off from what was once a self." Troubled by exhaustion and repeated stays in the hospital, she faced frustrating disruptions in her routines of writing, gardening, and seeing friends. She felt mocked by an essay in which she herself had termed old age an "ascension." Gradually, however, she returned to her insight from another perspective:

> The ascension is possible when all that has to be given up can be *gladly* given up—because other things have become more important. I panted halfway up the stairs, but I also was able to sit and watch light change in the porch for an hour and be truly attentive to it, not plagued by what I "ought" to be doing.[13]

"Other things" become more important. This is what we learn after we have been physically helpless. Slowing down enough to watch the light changing on a porch, rather than hastening to get things done, accords both with the rhythms of exhaustion and the need for repose.

A woman who had a painful disease in her teens writes about the awareness that has greeted her every morning since:

> I wake, and have for years now, overwhelmed by a sense of gratitude; it's like an sixth sense, like waking to the smell of smoke in a house or to the sound of a child's cry. It's a reckless feeling, unbidden as tears. . . . Gratitude, it seems after all, is the scar left me by my illness; I wake to run my fingers along its seam.[14]

DRY TEARS

In many respects, adult dignity makes us lonely. Children express their hurts and readily seek comfort from others, while we steel ourselves against our sorrows and pass the years with our most vulnerable feelings shielded from view. People know us by our defenses, by the social masks we don when we expect to be scrutinized. An eighty-five-year-old woman writes:

> At times I am a burden to myself. I wish I could let go and cry as a child cries.... As we get older, we cry less. We learn better and better how to inhibit our feelings, show self-control, how not to weep. Judging by my own feelings, however, I feel that I often do cry inside. That makes it much harder. My tears are dry.... Tears that are not shed go away slowly and return frequently. Such suffering I cannot adequately describe. I imagine that many old people in this world cry dry tears much of the time.[15]

Illness pulls us out of our adult solitude, to our embarrassment and our relief. We each retain the sensitivity of a five-year-old, but it takes a catastrophe—pain or sheer helplessness—for us to express ourselves directly as children do. The French philosopher Albert Camus writes, "In that race which daily hastens us toward death, the body maintains its irreparable lead."[16]

A seventy-eight-year-old woman managed to conceal her incapacitating back pain and depression from her adult children for more than a year. Each time they visited, she covered up the signs of her increasing frailty. Finally, her pain became so severe that she had to be hospitalized. There, the full extent of her suffering was exposed, and her family surrounded her with the solicitude she had feared. She writes:

> I used to think I would want and need no succor or pity at my ending. Now I hope that caretakers will be ten-

der with me, and that friends and relatives will follow my lead, touch me, scold me, tease me, laugh, cry, and rejoice with me. Why not? I don't always want to have to hide myself.[17]

This woman realized that she had carried forward from her youth a fierce independence that brooked no compromise. The pattern had remained safely entrenched throughout her adult life. Only debilitating illness had the power to compel her to alter an aspect of her character so fundamental.

Our weakest moments are often our most tender. Tears, bodily secretions and sounds all become part of a newly public domain, inspiring confidences that may never before have been risked. A sixty-two-year-old woman describes what she learned in the hours following a major operation:

They wheeled me back to my room and I was OK for an hour, but then I started to vomit. The nurse gave me a bed pan. I asked her to pull the curtain around my bed so my roommate wouldn't be looking right at me. It was awful. The nurse left, and I just vomited and vomited. I heard someone open the curtain, and there was my daughter. I told her to go away, that this was the worst time to visit. She said, "That's why I'm here." I was caught by another spasm, and she went to grab a wash cloth to wipe my face. Before I could stop her, she gave me some water so I could rinse my mouth. Another spasm came, and there I was, vomiting with her sitting right next to me. She kept rubbing my back. I asked her how she could stand it, that the smell was disgusting. She said, "It *is* disgusting," and we both started laughing. She stayed there all afternoon with me and we talked our heads off. It was such a relief to have her there, and it was one of the best talks we'd ever had.

At their outer reaches, shame and intimacy converge; we become closer to each other the more we lose our privacy. Holding on harder, trying not to let go, is the essence of desperation. The poet Elizabeth Bishop urges: "The art of losing isn't hard to master/ . . . practice losing farther, losing faster."[18] We eventually progress to a further kind of dignity, but not without first relinquishing several layers of privacy.

We are fortunate when an illness is so disruptive that we lose all means of clinging to our previous patterns. Once such longstanding boundaries are crossed, further liberties in a family's style of conversation and affection tend to follow. A physical therapist tells how a stroke led to the reconciliation of a father and son who had not spoken in years:

> My patient was a large man, and the dead weight of his stroke made it impossible for his tiny wife to move him at all. His son agreed to come over and learn how to do a wheelchair transfer, but he came in looking so hostile that I wanted to call off the whole thing. He didn't even say hello. I explained that he had to grip his father in a bear hug and then use a rocking motion to pivot him from the bed to the wheelchair. The son went over to the bed where his father was sitting and put his arms around him, just like I said. He got the rocking motion going, but then all of a sudden I realized that both of them were crying. It was the most amazing thing. They stayed like that for a long time, rocking and crying.

This father and son had not embraced since the son was a small boy. The sensation of being held by his son made the father cry, and the father's weeping moved the son to tears. Without the exigency of the stroke, they might never have dared to be different with each other.

Illness humbles us and makes more of us at the same

time. When our primitive needs move to the forefront of daily life, we are thrust back into dimensions of ourselves that may have been out of reach for years. A sixty-three-year-old woman describes what she discovered during surgery:

> I had to be awake during the operation. It was terrible, because I could hear the surgeon tinkling with his knives. I was so scared. All of a sudden, I felt someone take my arm and cradle it. I was too drugged to turn my head and see who it was. After a while, I realized they weren't going to let go. I couldn't believe it. This was someone's job, to hold onto me during the operation. I put my mind on that arm and that hand pressing on me. It was like a life preserver. I clung to that feeling for all I was worth. The oddest thing was that I didn't want it to end. The comfort, I mean, not the surgery. It felt so good to be held like that.

Recovering the yearnings of childhood is one of the chief recompenses of illness. After years of containment, these feelings are hugely responsive to small measures of relief and comfort. There is a simplicity in the sickbed that mirrors the simplicity and satisfaction of the cradle.

A sixty-year-old daughter of a woman with Alzheimer's disease describes how she soothes her mother when she wakes up and cries with fear in the middle of the night:

> I put my arms around her and hold her. I hold her as I held my children when they were small and afraid in the night; as, this summer, I hold my grandchildren. I hold her as she, once upon a time and long ago, held me. And I say the same words, the classic, maternal, instinctive words of reassurance. "Don't be afraid. I'm here. It's all right," . . . I mean these words. I do not understand them, but I mean them. Perhaps one day I will find out what I mean.[19]

Vulnerability evokes powerful feelings in both the sick and the well. We do not have to understand these feelings as much as we need to respond to them. Through our responses, we learn about the aspects of ourselves and our relationships that may have been concealed for years. We return to the truths we abandoned in childhood. In *Life Against Death,* Norman O. Brown observes, "What the child knows consciously, and the adult unconsciously, is that we are nothing but body. . . . Life is of the body and only life creates values; all values are bodily values."[20]

AT A LOSS FOR WORDS

Oliver Sacks, the neurologist and author, maintains that his style of practicing medicine was transformed after a leg injury forced him to endure months of helplessness in a hospital and then a nursing home:

> I came to realize, as did my patients, that there is an absolute and categorical difference between a doctor who *knows* and one who does not, and that this knowing can only be obtained by a personal experience of the organic, by descending to the very depths of disease and dissolution.[21]

Intellectual acknowledgment of one's ultimate fragility is no match for the yield of lived experience. We are always aware that we are vulnerable to illness, but we do not quite believe in its likelihood until it actually happens to us. Years after his leg healed, Dr. Sacks's patients continued to recognize him as someone marked by the experience of helplessness.

When someone who has not yet been personally initiated into the world of illness visits someone in a hospital or nursing home, the rift between health and illness is most pronounced. A man in his late sixties, the owner of a thriving business, told me:

> One of my best friends is in a nursing home. He had a stroke a few years ago. I've been to see him a few times, but I hate going. I don't know what to say when I see him, and he doesn't have much to say to me because his life is so empty there. It's awful. I don't want to go back, but how can I not go back? We've been friends for over thirty years. I can't just forget about him. So I should go, but I haven't in months. I feel terrible about it.

The layout of nursing homes compels us to walk through a wrenching silence on our way to the person we are visiting. The lobby and hallways are full of people sitting in wheelchairs, staring into space and not speaking to one another. By the time we reach our friend or relative's room, we may already feel strangled, wanting to flee the silence or to force the exuberance of the outside world into such a speechless place.

We have few ways to approach illness, except through the language of abhorrence. In *Medical Nemesis,* Ivan Illich writes, "Medical civilization is planned and organized to kill pain, to eliminate sickness, and to abolish the need for an art of suffering and of dying."[22] We find ourselves at a loss for words when standing at someone's bedside in a hospital or nursing home and believe that we are failing. A psychiatrist analyzes the subtle underpinnings of such encounters:

> Under all circumstances, a visit is an institutionalized and stylized affair. It has rules of conduct and sets of

expectations. It is a staged encounter with little sponta-
neity, and more often than not it is simply an exchange
of formalized cliches. Thus, a visit by a son or daughter to an aged parent may be regarded as an act of
comfort and support on the part of the visitor but as
an affliction by the one visited, or vice versa.[23]

We rush to arrange the flowers or report on the
weather, trying to cover our awkwardness with falsely cheerful banter. A nursing home staff member notes that infre-
quent visitors to her facility have the most difficulty bearing
what they see. She writes, "It is as though the observer himself stood there, revealed . . . and with unbordered empathy
comes flight." She goes on to claim that pity "creates a separation of witness and participant; by assuming a person is
absorbed in suffering, the witness prohibits them from participation in anything else."[24]

A nursing home resident who found a way to make her
visitors feel comfortable explains:

> I started asking my visitors to read my mail out loud to
> me or help me write letters. They didn't know what to
> do with themselves, and I was afraid they'd stop com-
> ing. So I put them to work. The company means a lot
> to me. They don't have to entertain me, do a dance for
> me—just be there. What matters to me is that they've
> bothered to come.

We who can walk away from the bedside and resume the
freedoms of the outside world must be careful not to judge
the ill person's situation on our terms. Inflated by good
health, our standards are likely to render our judgements
too severe and cause us to miss nuances of pleasure and
meaning. The very conditions which evoke our revulsion
may be all that someone has left of satisfaction.

The gap between witness and participant closes with proximity. We pull up a chair to the bedside and discover that our presence is the comfort, more than anything that we could have said. Once we get close enough to the illness to breathe it and feel it, we become acclimated to the odors and the humiliations. Reading, writing letters, watching television, or working on projects alongside the ill person converts a visit into a mutual experience. By suppressing our desire to flee, we learn that our silence is a kind of eloquence.

Following a burial, Jewish tradition prescribes the silent presence of others for seven days to "join the bereaved in his loneliness, sorrowfully to sit alongside him, to think his thoughts and to linger on his loss."[25] This same merging of feelings lessens the loneliness of someone who is grieving the loss of health and independence. Once ill people and those who minister to them accede to speechlessness, illness becomes permeable to solace.

A man faced with his own cancer diagnosis finally understood what his wife had needed from him when she was dying five years before: "Then I was tongue-tied. I did not know what to say. I could have rubbed her back every night, as the nurses did for me, but it never occurred to me then."[26] A woman who was hospitalized at the age of eighty for an eye operation explains:

> I knew the nurses by their hands. There was one with such delicate fingers that I cried a little when I heard her come on duty. She made me feel like she had all the time in the world. The others made me feel like a lump of flesh, like they had to get me out of the way as fast as they could. But those hands! I knew it was going to be a good day when she squeezed my arm in the morning. She would put a fresh gown on me and brush

my hair with such tenderness and patience. You can't imagine how much it meant to me, there in that strange place, to be touched like that.

Mercy most affects us when we are in the hospital or nursing home. We become primitive, hungry for touch and comfort. The rhythm of intake and outflow, of food and excrement, triggers our contact with the staff. After we push the call button, we wait. Time slows down as we listen to nurses' voices out in the hall and wonder what is taking precedence over our needs. It can seem that all we have been and done has come to nothing. In this situation, someone taking the time to heed our cravings and recognize our needs means more than we can say.

In the novel *Dad,* William Wharton portrays the plight of a son who moves in with his father in order to assist him with his progressive memory loss. Night after night, his disoriented father wanders the house, disturbing the son's sleep with his misadventures and agitations. The son becomes more and more exhausted. Finally, he comes up with a simple solution:

> I find it a great comfort to sleep with someone. Sleeping with another human is one of the great life pleasures, maybe even a necessity. I'm sure it's only recently humans have been sleeping alone. . . . Especially, asking children to sleep alone in the dark is cruel; time is different for a child, longer. And right now, Dad is like a child. I sleep with him. Small as he is, he seems monstrous. I've never slept with a man before. . . . The smell is different, the feel, the height of the shoulders, the breadth of chest, the over-all hardness, feeling of density; it's entirely another thing. . . . We sleep! He sleeps; I sleep! We sleep through the

night like mice. I never move and he doesn't either. God, it's nice![27]

We are not meant to keep illness separated from the rest of living. When we put off visits to friends and relatives, our thoughts return inexorably to our images of their situation. We cannot shed our awareness that their fate could just as easily be ours. Increasing rather than lessening our dread of the future, our avoidance deprives us of the very foreknowledge that would make the end of life less frightening. We do better to venture as far as we can into the territory of illness.

§

Not being isolated, not being in pain, and not yet being dead are privileges which we relish most after we endure loneliness, agony, and a glimpse of death. Under duress, the human capacity to make meaning out of the barest circumstances asserts itself. A man who watched his companion die of AIDS asks, "This burning away of the superfluous, the sheer pleasure of an ordinary afternoon—does anybody ever get taught these things by anything other than tragedy?"[28] If we do not resist its lessons, illness pulls us down to the level of sensate simplicity where true solace is possible.

From his hospital bed, a seventeen-year-old cancer patient yearned to look at the whole of the sky. His mother recorded her conversation with him a few days before his death:

When he awoke, I thought maybe the light was hurting his eyes. I started to lower the window blind.
"No, no!" He stopped me. "I want all the sky!"
He couldn't move (too many tubes), but he looked at that bright blue square with such love. The snow had

stopped and in its place we now had blazing, brilliant sunshine. "The sun," he said. "It was so good—"

The February afternoon grew dark. He grew more tired. After a while he whispered, "Do something for me? Leave a little early. Walk a few blocks and look at the sky. Walk in the world for me. . . ."[29]

FOUR

The Worth of the Past

We can stop to compose ourselves at any time. Composure is the result, not the precondition, of assembling the events of our lives into a meaningful whole. The word compose comes from the Latin root *pausare*, to rest, and the Greek *pauein*, to stop.[1] If we are fortunate, we get to take a long pause before the stop of death. When frailty or illness limits our external activities, we are given the opportunity to expand our reach into ourselves.

The French writer Marcel Proust sought repose in secluding himself from an active life at the age of thirty-four and gathering together his memories until he died twelve years later. George Painter, his biographer, writes:

> Proust believed, justifiably, that his life had the shape and meaning of a great work of art: it was his task to select, telescope and transmute the facts so that their universal significance should be revealed. . . . But though he invented nothing, he altered everything. His places and people are composite in space and time, constructed from various sources and from widely separate periods of his life.[2]

Our recollections are mosaics, composed of fragments of what we actually experience and arranged to suit our need for meaning. At each juncture, we decide what to reveal to others, what to keep for ourselves, and what to forget. The approach of death, more than any other urgency, summons our desire to determine the worth of the past.

This chapter enters into the pause that illness grants us. At the end of our lives, we are surrounded by our accumulated belongings as well as the sum of our memories. The long hours of lying in bed or being confined to home invite us to use the interlude to make order out of life's disarray. At this juncture, retrospection and introspection finally merge into a single quest for meaning: we recall the stories of our lives, and the stories tell us who we have been.

ACCUMULATIONS

Some people hoard the past. I have entered homes in which magazines, mail, and memorabilia filled every available surface: counters, tabletops, floors, shelves, chairs, and even windowsills. The hallways in these homes had been reduced to paths between shoulder-height piles, and the living rooms and bedrooms had forfeited all places to sit in preference to the stacks. I once asked a seventy-six-year-old owner of such a home why she was saving these things. She answered with some exasperation:

> Everyone asks me that. Those are good magazines. Why should I throw them out? I haven't read them all yet. Besides, if I throw some away, I might need them later and get mad at myself. You never know what you might need later, what might be important. And the old letters—I have every letter that anyone's ever sent

me. How can you throw out a letter someone's taken
the trouble to write?

To varying degrees, we all accumulate things as ap-
pendages of ourselves. We construct a world which is constantly within reach and which endures more reliably than
anything human. Things literally stand by us. Their constancy becomes all the more valuable when we move from
place to place, or when the rest of our lives seems to be in
flux.

In an essay, "Good-bye to Forty-Eighth Street," E. B.
White depicts his preparations to move out of a residence
that had contained the flux of his life for many years:

> For some weeks now I have been engaged in dispers-
> ing the contents of this apartment, trying to persuade
> hundreds of inanimate objects to scatter and leave me
> alone. It is not a simple matter. I am impressed by the
> reluctance of one's worldly goods to go out again into
> the world. . . . It is not possible to keep abreast of the
> normal tides of acquisition. A home is like a reservoir
> equipped with a check valve: the valve permits influx
> but prevents outflow. Acquisition goes on night and
> day—smoothly, subtly, imperceptibly. . . . Under ordi-
> nary circumstances, the only stuff that leaves a home is
> paper trash and garbage; everything else stays on and
> digs in.[3]

We gain palpable security from our possessions. One
daughter told me that she found hundreds of rolls of toilet
paper and packages of lightbulbs in her mother's basement
after her death. Another reported a closet full of more than
fifty brand-new pairs of the one shoe that did not hurt her
mother's feet. The owner of a used book store said that one
of her older customers buys books a shelf at a time, returning boxloads only when he can no longer close the door of

his apartment. A woman who befriended a seventy-seven-year-old Wyoming sheep herder describes his dwelling:

> Opening the door of his sheep wagon was to risk a bombardment of junk—chains, rusty wire, gunny sacks, broken cardboard cartons—none of it useable. His living space had been reduced to a few feet. Fred slept half sitting on the floor by the door, his mattress propped against these belongings whose bulk perhaps served as ballast against so many years alone.[4]

Many people have their closest relationships with things. The German critic Walter Benjamin suggests that "ownership is the most intimate relationship that one can have to objects." The longer we own our belongings, the more we belong to them. Benjamin asserts that the collector "dreams his way not only into a remote or bygone world, but at the same time into a better one in which . . . things are liberated from the drudgery of uselessness."[5] He cites the German word *aufheben,* which can be taken to mean preserve, elevate, or cancel. Collecting preserves the past while it elevates objects in value and cancels out their ordinary functions.

Accumulating and remembering are parallel phenomena, one external and the other internal. Yet both can be carried to an extreme. Some accumulators can be said to have concretized and embellished the ancient Greek art of remembering. In *The Art of Memory,* Frances Yates paraphrases the original instructions for this memory system:

> In order to form a series of places in memory . . . a building is to be remembered, as spacious and varied a one as possible, the forecourt, the living room, bedrooms, and parlours, not omitting statues and other ornaments with which the rooms are decorated. The

images by which the speech is to be remembered . . .
are then placed in imagination on the places which
have been memorized in the building. This done, as
soon as the memory of the facts requires to be revived,
all these places are visited in turn and the various de-
posits demanded of their custodians.[6]

In many cluttered homes, I have been told by the owners that they know where everything is and that any attempt
to rearrange their stacks in the interest of neatness would
destroy their retrieval system. Objects and places are tied
together in real instead of imagined houses, with the same
result: an extraordinary ability to recover what has been
stored. Yet for all their powers of retrieval, such people are
still thwarted by the dilemma of disposal.

We must all contend with the prospect that one day
our accumulations will be thrown away. The remembering
mind which confers value and order on things necessarily
disappears. The problem that accumulations pose is therefore nothing less than the problem of death.

A faithful diarist faces death with each blank page, by
deciding on a daily basis which experiences to record and
which to consign to the oblivion of forgetfulness. In *A
Book of One's Own: People and Their Diaries,* Thomas Mallon
writes:

> The accumulated past makes the shrinking future
> more bearable. . . . Time is the strongest thing of all,
> and the diarist is always fleeing it. He knows he will
> eventually be run to earth, but his hope is that his book
> will let each day live beyond its midnight, let it con-
> tinue somewhere outside its place in a finite row of
> falling dominoes. . . . My father never kept a diary, but
> he never threw away a canceled check, either. When he
> died a few years ago I came across thousands of them
> in perfect order in a series of shoeboxes.[7]

We all want some portion of our lives to "live beyond its midnight," yet selectivity is the only way to keep from amassing garbage. The labor of choosing what to keep and what to throw away is fundamental to creating anything of value. A diarist who fails to choose and instead tries to record everything on the page soon resembles the woman who saves everything in her house: when everything is valuable, nothing in particular is of worth.

The conflict between sentimental preservation and reasonable disposal is never more intense than when we must clean out the residence of someone who has died. Rescuing too many items only passes the burden onto our eventual heirs, while discarding someone's possessions makes us accomplices in the process of removal started by death. The writer Paul Auster chose to discard his father's possessions shortly after his funeral. He writes:

> If there was a single worst moment for me during those days, it came when I walked across the front lawn in the pouring rain to dump an armful of my father's ties into the back of a Good Will Mission truck. There must have been more than a hundred ties, and many of them I remembered from my childhood: the patterns, the colors, the shapes that had been embedded in my earliest consciousness, as clearly as my father's face had been. To see myself throwing them away like so much junk was intolerable to me, and it was then, at the precise instant I tossed them into the truck, that I came closest to tears.[8]

We do not take our disappearance lightly. It hurts to realize that most of what we cherish will someday be treated as garbage. Throwing away the memento of a loved one feels like we are consigning that person's memory to trash. A daughter describes the conflict she faces each time she comes upon her deceased mother's umbrella in storage:

I don't know why I'm saving it. It's old and dirty and torn, and yet I've taken it with me each time I've moved. It's been over twenty years since my mother died, yet I can't seem to throw it out. A few times already, I've held it over the dumpster, ready to drop it in, but I wasn't able to. It's crazy, because I never look at it, except when I go to get something else out of storage and there it is. Then I pick it up and look at it, and I can see my mother walking along with it like it was yesterday. She was never without it. I go through the same debate over and over again: should I keep it or throw it away? I always end up putting it back.

In one glance, this woman sees a useless object which she wants to discard and a precious fragment of her mother's life which she wants to preserve. Over time, our need to call up memories of someone wanes, but we resist the waning of this need as if it is a disloyalty and not a slow process of yielding. Saving a keepsake becomes a refusal to yield.

We need both recollection and relinquishment; hoarding the past is no better than shunning it. Partings from people and belongings are inevitable, yet this disengaging does not have to be heartless. In *The Duino Elegies,* Rainer Maria Rilke writes: "We live our lives, for ever taking leave."[9] The capacity to become unencumbered by the past lies in the nature of our leave-taking, not in cutting ourselves off from sentiment.

We thrive when we attain a flexible relationship with the past. After discovering that her son had put her grandfather's portrait under a crate in his basement, a seventy-one-year-old woman withstood a metamorphosis:

It was a shock, let me tell you. Something so important to me meant nothing to him. At first, I was hurt, insulted. Then I thought, there's only so many things you can hang onto. There's only so much space in a house. All of a sudden I pictured my things in his basement after I died, collecting dust. I suppose you could say part of me died at that moment. I started throwing things out. It's much easier than you think. You take a good, hard look and then dump it. You only keep what really matters. My son did me a favor.

RISKING RECOLLECTION

Biologically, only the future matters; the aim of all creatures is to go on living. The tasks of obtaining food, constructing nests and shelters, procreating, and feeding the young ensure the future. Unique to the human condition is the privilege and burden of a past. When our biological aims recede in prominence, what is most distinctive in us can finally gain ascendance. In *Time and the Art of Living,* Robert Grudin suggests that "memory should become a more and more important function of awareness, until it predominantly defines our individual identity."[10]

I once visited the apartment of ninety-eight-year-old man who had lost his right hand in a milling accident at the age of eighteen. His living room was empty except for a threadbare couch, and his linoleum floor had years of dirt layered upon it. There were no books or photographs, nor was there a television set. I asked him what he did all day:

Passing the time is no problem. I've had quite an interesting life. You see, when the saw took my hand, at that very moment, I knew that I would never marry and have children. Who would marry a man who couldn't support a family? I knew that I was going to have to live a different sort of life. I decided to have adventures, to travel all over the world and pick up work as I went along. I've lived just about everywhere. So now, every day, I decide on a certain piece of my life and try to remember everything that happened. I go back to a particular month and try to picture it, day by day if I can. You wouldn't believe how much comes back when you have nothing else to do. It's like watching a movie, because I've had so many adventures. The day goes by quickly. And I've had such a full life that I won't run out of things to remember, no matter how long I live.

This man displayed the artfulness of a Proust in his ability to adorn his present life with his past. Most of us cannot so readily dispense with disappointment or do without external comforts and distractions, but his inventiveness models a possibility. In *Letters to a Young Poet,* Rilke proposes the idea that we each possess in our past an inexhaustible storehouse of material for reflection and creativity. He advises a frustrated young poet:

> And even if you were in some prison the walls of which let none of the sounds of the world come to your senses—would you not then still have your childhood, that precious, kingly possession, that treasurehouse of memories? Turn your attention thither. Try to raise the submerged sensations of that ample past; your personality will grow more firm, your solitude will widen and will become a dusky dwelling past which the noise of others goes by far away.[11]

Many people insist that they find little value in going back over the past, even as their future shrinks and their past becomes their most extensive possession. Sorrow, regret, and guilt accompany their passage into their memories. Such people ruminate when they cannot sleep, captured by the ceaseless reiteration of all that remains unresolved. An eighty-eight-year-old woman writes, "When I could work, I could put other problems to the back of my mind, but now, grown out of all proportion, they occupy the dark hours of the night."[12]

In dread of such feelings, many use alcohol or attempt to submerge themselves in continual distractions. A man in his eighties recalls his evasions:

> After my wife died I started drinking—I started soon after her death but got into it a few months later. . . . It started small but soon grew. I was spending ten dollars or more a day on drink. They know me at every bar from here to the Avenue. I had a routine: start at one, move to the next, and back again when I was at the end. Between times, I'd ride the buses and travel around.[13]

Once he started drinking to cover his pain, this man was forced to keep on drinking. Spending time in bars limited him to the company of people who were incapable of extending themselves to him and shut out experiences which might have revived him.

Closing oneself off from significant parts of the past is a common self-protection. In a study of reminiscence among older people, the sociologist Peter Coleman found that one-third of those he interviewed preferred not to recall the past. A seventy-two-year-old man who had lost his wife two years before told Coleman that thinking of the past only made things harder for him: "It's not good to look back. It makes you more miserable than you have to be, you see."[14]

For years, the worth of the past may not be evident. The large, overriding story in a person's history may be obscured by apparently disjointed events. It can seem that one era of life has nothing to do with another, or that one phase directly contradicts another. Trying to discern a theme that makes sense or offers solace may seem fruitless.

One difficulty is that our most important stories have to be lived before they can be spoken. Freud suggests that we repeat painful parts of our past through our actions long before we are able to call them forth as actual memories. He notes that when someone reproduces an earlier event "not in his memory but in his behavior," he repeats it "without of course knowing that he is repeating it."[15] Once I listened, without saying a word, as a sixty-eight-year-old woman suddenly grasped the connections between different parts of her life:

> Since coming to this country, I've never lived anywhere more than a few years at a time. Things just bubble up inside me and I've got to go. It's been exhausting, let me tell you. I've had to start over more times than I can count. But now my arthritis is so bad, I've got to stay put. Things still bubble up just the same, but I talk it down. I've got no choice. Sometimes I sit for hours, not moving a muscle. I get so sad. You know what comes to me then? My family. I was very attached to them. Like a fool, I fell in love with a soldier and moved an ocean away. I had to freeze my heart to do it. I guess I haven't let myself melt till now. No wonder I've never sat still before. That's what's happening—I'm missing my family. They're all gone now, but I never missed them like this. No, not like this.

This woman's agitation gradually subsided in the following months. She began to recover the memories from which she had been exiled for decades. In restoring her past, she found relief from the pressure of feelings that had been too long contained.

Recalling earlier versions of ourselves is initially disquieting. In *The Uses of Reminiscence*, Marc Kaminsky notes, "The life review process is an ongoing one. Peace may be won, but it is usually something like a truce between re-

newed outbreaks of conflict."[16] Yet if we persist in the effort
to sort through and to make order of our experiences, we
may eventually come to peace with conflict itself. Once we
are able to discern value in the whole, we may begin to reconcile ourselves to the contradictory pieces that comprise a
life.

In *Man's Search for Meaning*, Viktor Frankl poses a contrast between two men, one who sadly and fearfully tears
each page from his wall calendar, and one who files each
page "neatly and carefully away . . . after first having jotted
down a few diary notes on the back." Of the second man, he
writes:

> He can reflect with pride on all the richness set down
> in these notes, on all the life he has already lived to the
> full. What will it matter to him if he notices that he is
> growing old? . . . What reason has he to envy a young
> person? For the possibilities that a young person has,
> the future that is in store for him? "No, thank you," he
> will think. "Instead of possibilities, I have realities in
> my past, not only the reality of work done and of love
> loved, but of suffering suffered."[17]

My contribution to my patients' lives is often to urge
them to risk recollecting themselves. In chemistry, resolution means breaking a compound apart into its components, and in optics, the term refers to rendering visible the
separate parts of a beam of light. In human life, we resolve
the problem of meaning by joining the disparate parts of
our lives together into a coherent whole.

TELLING STORIES

A seventy-nine-year-old man came into our clinic on the
seventieth anniversary of his father's death. When he

started sobbing out in the waiting room, I took him into my office. He told me this story as he cried:

> When I was nine, we lived near the railroad tracks, just up over the hill from them. I used to love running down to watch the trains go by. One day, I heard a train coming and I started running over there. At the top of the hill, I looked down and saw that someone had their foot caught in the tracks and was trying to pull loose. I ran over as fast as I could, but when I got closer I saw that it was my father. My father was stuck in those tracks. The train was getting so close, there was hardly any time. I couldn't move. I was so afraid. It was like I was trapped in molasses. The ground was shaking, and the whistle got louder and louder. He kept pulling on his leg, but the train killed him, it killed him, and I was right there.

Each time this man looked up at me, he saw his story reflected in my face. The desperation of that nine-year-old boy was mine, as if the accident were happening all over again that morning. The more I suffered there in the room with him, the louder he cried. His face became so red and his breathing so choked that I was afraid he would die from telling the story. Eventually, his pain reached a crescendo and then subsided.

This was our first meeting. In the following weeks, he showed me his collection of train books and other railroad mementos that had been entombed for years along with his terrible memory. He wanted me to savor each of these items with him, which he displayed with the enthusiasm of a young boy. He died a few months later, at ease with himself and his memories.

Convergences of remembrance and emotion brook no postponement. When feelings bound to the past are suddenly emancipated, we need someone to take the time to hear us out. Had I been too hurried for more than one sentence, "I saw my father killed by a train when I was nine," this man would not have attained the resolution he was seeking before he died.

This inclination to return to the beginning to make an ending arises in every form of human expression. We read novels for the resolution of the initial themes, and we listen to music with an ear toward the completion of what was set in motion with the first few notes. Victor Zuckerkandl, a music theorist, explores the yearning for a satisfying melodic ending:

> There is no escaping the octave structure of the tonal world. Here every movement which is not prematurely interrupted must with inevitable necessity return to its starting point; either it turns back and so returns of its own will, as it were, or it goes on in the same direction and runs into the octave. . . . Our satisfaction is . . . experiencing the incomplete becoming complete and the universal law of symmetry fulfilled.[18]

The process of attaining completion may not be as orderly in life as it is in music and literature, but the striving for symmetry is the same. A recollection plays out the original experience and changes it, just as an octave both repeats the beginning note and alters it. Peter Brooks, a literary theorist, points out that "an event gains meaning by its repetition, which is both the recall of an earlier moment and a variation of it."[19] We construct endings by returning to familiar events and making more of them than we did before.

In telling our most painful stories to someone else, we simultaneously repeat our suffering and allow it to evolve into something we can bear. At first, a listener's compassion can be so evocative that it seems to worsen sorrow: "Stop being so nice to me—You're making me cry." A sympathetic listener brings out our pain in full force. Yet when someone receives what we are feeling and remembering, a progression is set in motion that can lead to repose.

A caring listener propels our stories by helping us select what we need to say out of the vast range of things that could be said. In *Every Person's Life Is Worth a Novel,* Erving Polster depicts a kinship between novelists and therapists. He argues that they use "the same creative selection process" in highlighting an individual's key experiences and providing "leverage for the emerging dramas." Claiming that "incoherence is often at the root of personal malaise," he suggests that therapists must remain alert for fundamental stories when they emerge and encourage the sense of completion that comes from the telling of such stories.[20]

We all desire a satisfying ending, to have our lives culminate in something that makes sense. Sense-making requires that the disparate parts of our lives fit together into one whole, comprehensive story. In *The Sense of an Ending,* Frank Kermode insists that such consonance is necessary for the attainment of meaning. He writes:

> We humanly do not want it to be an indeterminate interval between the *tick* of birth and the *tock* of death. . . . We look for a fullness of time, for beginning, middle and end in concord. For concord or consonance really is the root of the matter, even in a world which thinks it can only be a fiction. . . . We need, and provide, fictions of concord.[21]

In their interviews with older people, researchers are confirming the prevalence of this need for expression and cohesion. In *The Ageless Self: Sources of Meaning in Late Life,*

Sharon Kaufman observes that, above all, we seek continuity in our recollections "so that a familiar and unified sense of self emerges in old age."[22] The gerontologists Morton Lieberman and Sheldon Tobin interviewed eighty-five people who were on the verge of entering nursing homes. Consistently, these people sought a theme in their lives to account for what was happening to them. Lieberman and Tobin conclude from their research that reminiscence serves "to resolve a critical dilemma posed by the issues of old age and leads not to serenity but rather to stability."[23]

No one lives without accumulating stories. Language itself makes us the subject around whom all else is predicated. Before we say a word, grammar involves us in a past, present, and future. In *The Human Condition,* Hannah Arendt asserts that "action and speech are indeed the two activities whose end result will always be a story with enough coherence to be told."[24]

The opportunity to voice memories to a person who both cares and understands is the most satisfying kind of completion. Story-telling is therefore far more valuable than it may seem when helpers have so much else to do on an ill person's behalf. Realizing that such stories allow us to make an ending and find worth in the past elevates remembering and listening to their actual stature.

Before she died of cancer, a young nurse wrote an anonymous plea to her colleagues in a national nursing journal:

> You slip in and out of my room, give me medications and check my blood pressure. . . . Don't run away— wait—all I want to know is that there will be someone to hold my hand when I need it. I am afraid. Death may get to be a routine to you, but it is new to me. You may not see me as unique, but I've never died before. . . . I have lots I wish we could talk about. It really would not

take much more of your time because you are in here quite a bit already.[25]

§

Doris Kearns, a biographer of Lyndon Johnson, interviewed him at his ranch on a daily basis during the last year of his life. She recalls:

> As two heart attacks ravished him . . . he became less guarded, almost as though, despite all his defenses, he had to tell his tale to someone in bits and pieces before it was too late. . . . He would awaken me at five in the morning because he could not sleep and had to talk. His sense that he was dying unlocked his earliest memories.[26]

The approach of death overcomes even the most staunch resistance to looking backward and looking inward. We widen our solitudes by esteeming our memories and making use of them, instead of hoarding them, disregarding them, or keeping them to ourselves.

FIVE _____

Parents Dying

It can take a lifetime to know our parents in their
full humanness. A woman at midlife writes:

> I think of my mother walking with my grandmother,
> annoyed because suddenly she wasn't walking fast
> enough, her eyes searching for the sky in utter impa-
> tience. Years later, me, walking with my mother, want-
> ing to sprint and having to walk slower because she
> couldn't keep up and my eyes starting for the sky and
> stopping halfway there, remembering my mother's
> look of years ago. And now, my personal stab. Always
> walking faster than my kids and and now my kids mov-
> ing those long legs of theirs past me and my rushing to
> keep up.[1]

As we get older, our respect for our parents' achievements
increases, as does our sympathy for their disappointments
and failures. The more our own lives twist in unexpected
and humbling directions, the more we realize that our parents had been similarly buffeted. We become our parents'
retrospective peers, seeing more of them as we attain each
decade. When our physical capacities wane and our own
death draws near, we tend to comprehend our parents as
never before.

While they were dying, many of my patients needed to tell me the stories of their parents' deaths, as if past and present were merging in a sudden flood of understanding. They recalled all that they did and did not do on their parents' behalf, finally grasping the meaning of their actions and their omissions.

To be fully understood, frailty has to be lived rather than merely witnessed. In *The Loneliness of the Dying,* Norbert Elias explains, "It is not easy to imagine that one's own body, which is so fresh and often so full of pleasant feelings, could become sluggish, tired and clumsy. One cannot imagine it and, at bottom, one does not want to."[2] Many of the realizations that rush upon us at the end are simply not attainable earlier in life.

In this chapter, three angles of vision are depicted: when our parents need our help prior to their deaths, the period after they die, and the time of life when we ourselves are nearing death. The nature of our insights changes, as does the degree of our willingness to scrutinize what we are able to discern. This progression is one of the most fruitful, yet least examined, aspects of aging and dying.

A DIFFERENT LIGHT

In *Honor Thy Father and Mother,* Gerald Blidstein argues that old age is the focal point of the commandment. He states, "Indeed, it is this period of the relationship that is perhaps the most difficult and, at the same time, the most significant."[3] This commandment is the only one of the ten which specifies a consequence: "that thy days may be long upon the land" (Exod. 20:12). Why honoring our parents is linked to this outcome is not immediately evident from the commandment itself, nor is it always evident in the living of our lives.

The duty to honor parents is most perplexing when parents have given their children few reasons to honor them. Parents who were neglectful or abusive when their children were young tend to incur resentment rather than loyalty. A forty-nine-year-old son describes his dilemma:

> I've resented my mother for so long, I can't imagine how else to be with her. I never tell her anything—just superficial things—so it would be strange to have a real conversation with her all of a sudden. Ever since Dad died, there's been times when she's tried to get something going with me, but I changed the topic. It's fine that she wants to be close, now that she needs me, but where was she when I really needed her?

Adult children in this position frequently insist that they have little to gain from putting aside their bitterness and attempting reconciliation. They retaliate through silence when their parents try to explain themselves or attempt to rectify old wrongs. They refuse to grant their parents the kind of sympathy that was not given to them as children. In *Adults and Their Parents in Family Therapy*, Lee Headley reports that adult children commonly insist that "there is a rigid and settled relationship between themselves and their parents . . . and that their parents will continue being the same kind of persons, making the same kind of moves that they have for years."[4]

Unbeknownst to their adult children, many older parents find that their willingness to explore the past increases the closer they get to the end of their lives. If illness then heightens their emotional expressiveness, as well as compelling them to depend on their children for help, an uncharacteristic need for disclosure and resolution may be unleashed. Over time, their desire to change previous patterns may far surpass that of their adult children. A forty-two-year-old man told me:

> A long time ago, I wrote my father off. I figured once a drunk, always a drunk. It was a lot less disappointing than trying to act like I really had a father. But when he got sick, the doctor told him he'd have to quit drinking or die. So he quit. And now I have a father, or at least a man who keeps trying to act like I'm his son. It's hard for me to believe that this man is my father. He's not making excuses any more. He's telling me straight out how messed up his own father was, and how scared he was when I was born because he didn't know what to do, how to be a good father. I still can't believe that this is the same man. All he ever showed me before was a lot of bluster. Now he's trying to show me what was underneath. It's hard for me to buy it.

As children, the chief illusions we project upon our parents are that they know what they are doing and that they have control over what happens. It does not occur to us that what appears to be inflexibility may actually be a cover for confusion, or what comes out as anger may stem from anxiety, or what seems to be neglect and a lack of concern may be the consequence of depression. All of this can only make sense later, if we allow them to account for themselves and to acknowledge the extent to which their actions stemmed from their own weaknesses.

The more hurtfully our parents treated us as children, the more crucial it is for us to try to ascertain the wounds of their upbringing. Otherwise, their weaknesses become holes into which we pointlessly pour our resentment. Every one of their failures has a story behind it, a history which has been carried forward and re-expressed. To learn their history is to see our parents as people, rather than to react blindly against them and risk replicating their hurts in our own lives.

Turning the furor of our reactions into a reasonable quest for understanding is made easier when we are granted full access to our parents' histories. A man who spent a great deal of his boyhood around his father's mother recalls how deeply he benefitted from hearing her stories of his father's boyhood. He writes:

> How can a boy act out his rage when he knows the cause of it, knows that this father and his father's father before him suffered the same rage? How can a boy's view of his parents not be inevitably altered when each week he hears more of their story, is forced to see them in the context of *their* struggle for happiness?[5]

No one lives without making mistakes and incurring regrets, yet we all hope to be worthy of regard in the end. In *Outliving the Self,* John Kotre celebrates the occasions for intergenerational understanding that result from parents surviving into an extended old age. He notes that "never have so many generations in families been alive at the same time," leading to "new opportunities for reworking and repairing relations between parents and children."[6]

After her mother's eighty-six-year-old mother came to live with them, a twenty-three-year-old granddaughter observed:

> Having Grandma in our house has brought me closer to my mother and forced me to see her in a different light. Mother is a daughter to a woman, too, just like me, but I had never understood the force of this relationship in her life until now. I see my mother more as

a person now, not just my mom, because I've seen her in the vulnerable role of child. . . . Grandma is part of our family now. She's not some distant relative we see only occasionally, but an everyday part of our lives. We see her strengths and weaknesses and share her good days and bad. We witness her aging and find affirmation for our own.[7]

We are all children of parents, yet the ability to picture our parents as children can easily elude us. This daughter is witnessing firsthand the shortcomings in her grandmother which were hurtful to her mother as a child. Like nothing else, such glimpses across generations permit us to comprehend those who shaped us and ultimately ourselves.

The family therapists Ivan Boszormenyi-Nagy and Geraldine Spark present numerous cases in which assisting parents during their time of frailty spurs discoveries in parents, adult children, and grandchildren. They cite one case in which a young grandson expressed his family's most important insight:

The child's mother was saying that her aged mother was slipping. The maternal grandmother purchased two coats and kept asking people in her apartment building which coat was more attractive. The grandson, age thirteen, turned to his mother and said, "It is very simple. Tell grandma which coat you think she looks best in and then take the other coat back to the store for her. That is what she always used to do for you!"[8]

The notion of reciprocity, of being helped and then helping in return, appeals to our basic need for balance and order. When children watch their parents take time out of their busy lives to help their parents, they learn that devotion can persist even when it is inconvenient. As the Talmudic scholar Rabbi Saadiah Gaon observes, "Children should realize that if they regret the longevity of their parents, they will actually be regretting their own future longevity."[9]

Illness also opens up fresh areas of interchange. In the course of assisting our parents, we mingle in the details of their daily lives in ways that may not have been permitted since adolescence or may never before have been risked. Opportunities arise thereby for correcting old misconceptions as well as for incurring new irritations. Former conflicts may flare up with enough force to propel our finally working them out. A forty-nine-year-old son was stunned when his father suddenly broke out of a longstanding pattern:

> My father was always the biggest stickler on earth when it came to his checkbook. He never let anyone near it, not even my mother. In his eighties, his hand tremor got really bad, but he still insisted on paying all his bills himself. One day, out of the blue, he called me up and asked me to come over to help him write out checks. I couldn't believe it. I was incredibly nervous when I sat down next to him to do it. I handle million-dollar budgets for my company, and yet my hand started to shake for a lousy checkbook. I guess I wanted to please him, or maybe it was that I felt so honored that he was finally trusting me.

His father's trust was sweeter to this son than his achievement in the corporate world. Also, his father had the opportunity to see how large he still loomed in his son's life, despite his son's having garnered every external success.

Extending leniency to our parents gives us hope that someone will do the same for us when we reach this posi-

tion of physical need and spiritual reckoning. Even fum-
bled efforts at helpfulness and reconciliation are significant for the hope they instill and the example they set. A
man in his seventies who became close to his father shortly
before his death at the age of ninety-four recalls, "I told him
I loved him. I had never before articulated that love, nor he
to me. . . . How lucky I was to have him live so long."[10] Hope
is the essence of the commandment to honor our parents,
making the prospect of living a long life less frightening.

THE USES OF REGRET

In many respects, we cannot fully see our parents as people
until after they die. Then, their physical presence no longer
distracts us, and the consequences of making judgments
seems much less dire. Death finally extricates us from these
relationships, unmasking our parents' separateness and humanness. In *The Anatomy of Dependence,* Takeo Doi describes
his own experience:

> Following the death in rapid succession of both my
> parents and the consequent severing of my bonds with
> them, I became aware of them for the first time as inde-
> pendent *persons,* where hitherto their existence was
> real to me only insofar as they were my own par-
> ents. . . . I felt an intolerable sense of regret. If only, I
> told myself, I had done this or that. . . . And though I
> knew that none of my regrets could reverse what had
> happened, yet still for some time I could not make my-
> self cease regretting.[11]

The word regret derives from the Old English *gretan,* to
speak to, or to call out.[12] We return through memory to

events that had been previously unclear and re-greet them with the knowledge we have gained since these events transpired. In her adolescent diaries, the psychoanalyst Karen Horney records how she was suffused with self-reproach after her mother's death "for the countless unkindnesses one did her, large and small, the torment that this can never be made good." She broods relentlessly as she looks back at her mother's last days, seeing in retrospect all that she could have done on her mother's behalf and carrying a "feeling of guilt that will always remain and that should teach me to become kinder toward the living."[13]

We are always able to see farther looking back than we can in the crush of the present. After his father died, the Japanese writer Yasushi Inoue became aware for the first time of how much he resembled him. He writes, "I would feel him inside me at odd moments," noticing that the ways he performed ordinary actions, such as putting on his garden slippers, mirrored his father's gestures exactly. He describes a particularly stirring moment of "slipping into Father's way of thinking":

> When working I frequently get up from my desk to sit on a wicker chair on the veranda, letting my thoughts wander at random, with no connection to the work at hand. At those times I always fix my gaze on the old Chinese ash tree, which has branches spreading out in all directions. One day I recalled that Father also looked out at the branches of a tree as he sat in his wicker chair on the veranda in our country home. I felt then as if I were staring into a deep pool in front of me. I was overawed by the realization that Father had lost himself in thought in the same way. With feelings like these, the image of Father as a distinct and individual human being formed in my mind. I began to see him and talk with him frequently.[14]

Impelled by the fervor of their regret, many people find that they need to express all that remained unspoken at the time their parents died. In *The Orphaned Adult,* Rabbi Marc Angel marvels at the number of people who claim to hold conversations with deceased parents. He suggests that many "can actually feel the presence of their parents within them."[15] These dialogues often progress further than had been possible in life, since internal conversations are not constrained by the perils of actual communication.

Anger, in particular, has to play itself out before we can be released from it. A woman who was turning forty just as her mother died at eighty-one writes:

> Since my mother's death, I have been dreaming about her constantly. In these dreams I am confronted by her return from the grave. I awake upset and appalled by the anger expressed through the dreams. Well, I tell myself, I was often angry with her in life, why not in death? . . . While she and I argued most of our lives together over who or what we thought the other should be, at the end it was impossible to fight her. She couldn't fight back.[16]

Anger at the dead feels unseemly, but its force is rarely diminished by the perishing of its target. The work of resolution continues through every available means. In *Against the Grain: Coming Through Mid-Life Crisis,* David Maitland refers to his own efforts to see his parents as people, to be "free to honor them, and be somewhat free from them." He notes, "As long as I wished they had been other than they were . . . I was hopelessly trapped in my refusal to embrace the significant people of my own story."[17]

Emotions activated by a parent's death often take on a life of their own, evolving as we evolve. One woman needed to reach her sixties before she was able to admire her father:

"I began to know Father after his death. My own struggles with pain, with defeat, help me to know my father and to love him."[18] Another woman found that her father's death from a heart attack when she was forty-two kept on affecting her powerfully for years, changing the way she conducted her relationships and handled her aspirations:

> I learned that the most important thing in life is death. He was gone. I could never talk to him again. Before that, I didn't understand how serious life is. I wasted time and threw away chances to do things, thinking I could get everything done later. Since he died, I haven't had any patience for chatter. I get up and leave when my friends start talking about nothing. I can't get it out of my mind that one day it's all over. I think about how he just disappeared and I make sure I say what I want to say and do what I want to do.

The time remaining to us after our parents die becomes both more lonely and more lucid. A woman who was thirty-six when her mother died writes: "When a parent goes, half of [our] innocence goes, too. It gets ripped away. Something, someday will replace that innocence, maybe something more useful, but we cannot know what, or how soon, and while we wait, it hurts."[19]

The waiting is often rewarded expansively. Lily Pincus, a family therapist, observes that virtually all the adult children in her practice experienced "an upsurge of growth, a freeing of their own potential" as part of their bereavement. She cites the case of a passive man who became strong and efficacious after his father's death: "Suddenly he was the man of the house and what he said was law."[20] In *Memories, Dreams, Reflections,* Jung admits that after his father died "a bit of manliness and freedom" awoke in him.[21]

A woman in her forties compares her response to her

mother's death when she was nineteen with her present wisdom:

> It was very cold the night my mother died. She was a
> little older than I am today. . . . I knew that in the years
> following that January night I had been numb with
> fear at some simple truths: that I was going to have to
> find a way to earn a living, make a decision about what
> I wanted to do and how to go about doing it, find a
> home and make it my own. That was the only response
> I could find to the scent of death sticking to my clothes,
> rising from my hair. The house in which my mother
> had sickened and drawn near to death was sold not
> long after she died, and so in every sense I was adrift. I
> felt orphaned, cut off from the past. It was many years
> before I would know that I had found both feelings lib-
> erating.[22]

We cannot rush these discoveries. They are the consequence of living, not thinking. We can hasten to ask questions of surviving relatives, piecing together blurry aspects
of the past, but true forgiveness and growth arise with the
passage of time and the infusion of new experiences. A
woman who lost her sister and her father within a few
months of each other was unable to grasp this period of her
life until several years later: "Even the most painful losses
. . . have freed and strengthened me. I have had to give up
nostalgia and guilt to see this. . . . Acceptance keeps you
waiting, and then comes all at once. It is exuberant and generous, not dull and sluggish like loss."[23]

Of all the emotions left behind by bereavement, guilt
displays the most persistance. Often the only liberation is to
admit out loud the wrongs we think we committed, testing
them against another person's experience. In *The Summer of
the Great-Grandmother,* Madeleine L'Engle describes how she

managed to comfort a friend who was overwhelmed with guilt long after her mother died:

> I said that we all, all of us without exception, have cause for guilt about our parents, and that I had far more cause than she. Then I heard myself saying, "I don't think real guilt is ever much of a problem for us. It's false guilt that causes the trouble." . . . When I try to be the perfect daughter, to be in control of the situation, I become impaled on false guilt and become over-tired and irritable. It is only by accepting real guilt that I am able to be free of guilt.[24]

Guilt that demands perfection is relentless, while guilt that allows room for weakness subsides over time. Only when we stop holding ourselves to impossible standards can we start to relinquish the burden of our inevitable omissions and errors. In the long run, our flawed performance does not matter as much as the sincerity of the efforts we exerted.

Regret provokes our attainment of hindsight and incites our search for more. The stronger our regret after our parents' deaths, the more we can be assured that our wisdom has grown. Eventually, our self-knowledge and our understanding of our parents may expand to the point that it becomes possible to forgive ourselves and to grant our parents an unconditional right to their shortcomings. A man who was thirty-one when his mother died writes:

> The fourteen months of my mother's illness were the most physically and emotionally demanding period of my life. . . . I'm not at all convinced that I did a good job of looking after [her], or that I always acted selflessly, or that I understood the consequences of my choices; and I certainly don't believe that I made all the right decisions. . . . When it was over, I was ex-

hausted in more ways than I thought possible. But I
had done what I needed to do. Somehow, it was important and good to have done it.[25]

SECOND SIGHT

Our parents die twice: first, during their actual dying, and
again when we face our own death. After her stroke, the
writer May Sarton found that she could not get thoughts of
her mother out of her mind:

> I lie around most of the afternoon, am in bed by eight,
> and there in my bed alone the past rises like a tide,
> over and over, to swamp me with memories I cannot
> handle. . . . My mother dies again, and again I have to
> face that I did not have the courage to sit with her,
> which is what she needed.[26]

I have sat by the bedsides of many ill people who
needed to recount detailed memories of their parents' last
days. Specific scenes and conversations were coming back
to them with extraordinary vividness, triggered by their
own experience of helplessness. In our sickbeds, we tend to
relive the period during which our parents were in the
same position, revising our memories in accordance with
the knowledge we are so rapidly gaining.

One seventy-nine-year-old woman recalls her mother's
dogged self-reliance, belatedly respecting her for her way of
handling the dilemmas of dependency:

> My mother had nine children, but she refused to live
> with any of us. We did some of her errands, but she
> hardly let us help her at all. I was mad at her, because I
> thought it was foolish pride. Now I know what she was
> doing. It's hard to depend on your children, and it's

hard not to. You have your pride, but you need the help. It's a fine line. When I hear myself saying "no, thanks" to my daughter, I know what was going through my mother's mind back then.

As our physical powers decline, many of our adaptations and concessions are not visible to others. One by one, we exchange our standards of dignity for necessary security, but those who assist us may have no idea of the inner sacrifices these compromises entail. On the surface, our actions may appear to be foolish or obstinate, especially as we resist sensible offers of help and hold back as long as we can from each successive loss of autonomy.

Much of what seemed unreasonable at the time that we took care of our parents may suddenly make sense when we get close to the end of our lives. We may reverberate with the same worries and anxieties that we once scorned as irrational. A fifty-nine-year-old woman in the end stages of cancer admits, "I do what I was so angry at Mother for doing. Wasting the perfectly good present in fear about the future. . . . Worry is fantasy, it's imagining what may not ever be. Mine is a little realistic, though. But wasn't hers?"[27]

In light of our helplessness, we may recall favors we were too tired to perform, favorite foods we did not bother to prepare, and most regretfully, harsh words which we failed to suppress during moments of exasperation. But just as clearly as we realize what we did wrong, we gain a tangible understanding of what we did right. A woman who was seventy-one when her mother died at ninety explains:

> My mother was in a nursing home twelve years before she died. I had to take two buses to get there, so the whole trip took five hours. For all those years, I went twice a week. I hated going, but I went. People said I was nuts. But now I know what my visits meant to her.

> You have no idea what loneliness really is, until you get shut in like this. Now I know how it feels. I look back and I'm so glad that I was crazy enough to do that for my mother.

Once our own powers slip, we understand how raw life can get. We realize how deeply even our misdirected efforts must have been appreciated, and what a large difference our small acts of kindness must have made. In her novel *Memento Mori,* Muriel Spark writes: "How primitive . . . life becomes in old age, when one may be surrounded by familiar comforts and yet more vulnerable to the action of nature than any young explorer at the Pole. And how simply the physical laws assert themselves, frustrating all one's purposes."[28]

A man who had a heart attack at the age of sixty lay in the intensive care unit and could think only of his father:

> I keep picturing my father lying on the living room couch. I was eleven when he had his stroke and seventeen when he died. So that's how I knew him: paralyzed, trapped on a couch, lying there like I'm lying here, not knowing what's going to happen. Now I know what was on his mind, why he had nothing to say to me. He was afraid. You feel like your body could self-destruct at any second and there's nothing you can do about it. You feel helpless, cheated, terrified. He was so silent, it always hurt me. All of these years, I had the wrong idea. I'm so glad I've lived long enough to find this out.

This man became more and more joyous during his recuperation, spending hours revising his view of the past. For five decades, he had carried the shame of believing himself unworthy of his father's respect. Now he was able to enter into his father's silence from the inside and see how intense must have been his yearning to participate in his young son's life.

The deaths that we know most intimately accompany us to the end of our lives. In *Love's Executioner,* Irvin Yalom notes, "I have always felt that the way one faces death is greatly determined by the model one's parents set. The last gift a parent can give to children is to teach them, through example, how to face death with equanimity."[29] A seventy-two-year-old woman took care of her frail mother for five difficult years before she died:

> My mother died with a radiant look on her face. It took away my fear of death. As I get older, I think of her face more often, and this is how I picture myself dying.

So much becomes clear from the vantage point of frailty and helplessness that we have to rethink our lives in these terms. In a sickbed, we become equal to our parents as never before: equally vulnerable to dissolution. Recognition of this stark equality can supercede even a lifetime of differences. We may end up filling our parents' shoes exactly.

§

Acceptance of our parents tends to culminate at the end of our lives, when our circumstances are most humbling and our view of ourselves encompasses the full import of our past. We may finally be able to forgive our parents for their oversights and failings. In *Identity and the Life Cycle,* Erik Erikson suggests that full spiritual health arises when one attains an "acceptance of one's own and only life cycle" and a "new different love of one's parents, free of the wish that they should have been different."[30]

SIX

Unlived Life

The parts of ourselves that we neglect lie in wait for us, like an accusation. More than any other influence, illness fosters our recognition of unlived life. We become detached from the life we had been living and see its presumptions. A woman whose husband had a stroke just as they were about to depart on a cross-country trip speaks her mind:

> I'm so angry. Look at us. Instead of seeing America, we're prisoners. Sure, he couldn't help the stroke, but we could have gone on this trip years ago. There was always something at his job that just couldn't wait. Year after year, he gave me the same excuse. So here we are stuck. If the trip had been behind us already, I think I could have gotten through this. I would've had something to remember, to think back on. As it is, I have nothing. I feel cheated. That's the truth of it. And now he's a helpless man with a bitter wife.

Many clinicians measure the worth of therapy according to how much of the lifespan is ahead for enacting the changes that therapy might provoke. As a result, they believe that work with younger or healthier clients is more valuable than work with those who are aged or ill. Weary of such attitudes, a gerontologist protests that we "think of the young in terms of growth and change, but . . . no matter how much research has been done to demonstrate otherwise, we still hold little belief in the creative potentialities of the older person."[1]

This chapter surveys our opportunities for reclaiming unlived life once dire circumstances are upon us. In my clinical work, I have found that the transformations achieved by people facing serious illness or advanced age tend to be far more dramatic than those attained by people still caught up in the business of living. In "Frailty and Strength: The Dialectic of Aging," Sally Gadow asserts, "[Frailty] is itself an intense experience and brings with it new life."[2] The very constraints that illness imposes compel us to confront what is incomplete in ourselves.

A MATTER OF LIFE AND DEATH

The sooner we begin to live fully, the easier it is to accept becoming ill or growing old. A gerontologist claims that we "take ourselves with us as we grow older," stating, "how we live now, what our attitudes are toward living, growing, and aging, will be the most influential factors in determining how we age."[3] Yet prior to getting sick, few people live in terms of achieving a satisfied ending.

A fifty-eight-year-old woman was found to have a large tumor on her lung. Told that she had only a few months to live, she became overwhelmed with regret for her years of smoking. She pleaded with her thirty-six-year-old son to stop his own two pack a day habit. At her deathbed, he swore he would stop, but he resumed smoking a few months after she died. He describes his bewilderment at his own behavior:

After seeing what my mother went through, I can't believe that I can light up a cigarette. She hated to die so
young, to miss seeing her grandchildren grow up. She
hated getting to be so helpless. She had to gasp for air
at the end like she was drowning. It was horrible, and
here I am, hooked again, maybe worse than before. It
doesn't make any sense. I've got kids, a wife, a good
job. And every time I take out a cigarette, I see my
mother's face with the oxygen tube in her nose. I can
hear her again, begging me to stop. So what is it going
to take? Do I have to get cancer first?

Illness gives us the time and the impulsion to face ourselves. After learning that he had cancer, a man in his fifties
allowed himself to sit still for the first time in his adult life.
He told his physician, "I never had time to stop and look at
myself. I raced about never giving a thought where I was
racing to in such a hurry. When I got sick, it somehow
seemed all right to tuck myself up under the covers and
think about these things."[4]

In *The Conduct of Life,* Lewis Mumford recalls holding a
seminar for a group of educators, many of whom had
achieved eminence in their field of study. He asked them
"how many spent as much as half an hour a day in complete
solitude, with no outside interruption." One participant
shyly admitted that he took time each day to pray, but the
rest stated that "they were on the go from whenever they
rose to when they went to bed again." Mumford writes:

Too many of us wait for an illness . . . to entertain [sol-
itary] moments; and though a long quiet convales-
cence may sometimes bring an illumination that will
radically change the course of a life, we should not depend on such accidents to make a timely reorientation
possible. A half hour of solitude, detached and
"empty"—that is essential for a new beginning.[5]

Emptiness is an experience we tend to flee in Western cultures, rather than allowing it to ground us. A woman who was diagnosed with lupus while in her early thirties writes: "I had never before appreciated inactivity. I always had to be doing something, even if it were just knitting or reading—getting to that row in the pattern, or going as far as the next chapter. . . . It was during these afternoons that I felt my soul opening and strengthening, like a muscle . . . I saw the healing goodness of inactivity, silence."[6]

Virginia Woolf suggests that it is precisely when we have an abundance of stillness that we are able to resume our fullest possession of both the present and ourselves:

> The past only comes back when the present runs so smoothly that it is like the sliding surface of a deep river. Then one sees through the surface to the depths. In those moments I find one of my greatest satisfactions, not that I am thinking of the past; but it is then that I am living most fully in the present. For the present when backed by the past is a thousand times deeper. . . . To feel the present sliding over the depths of the past, peace is necessary. The present must be smooth, habitual.[7]

Many people bypass silence entirely as they run through their lives, meeting up with it again only when their doings are forcibly stilled. In *The World of Silence*, Max Picard claims that "silence is the only phenomenon today that is 'useless.' " He points out that it cannot be exploited for profit and is therefore thought to have no value. He writes, "Yet there is more help and healing in silence than in all the 'useful things.' . . . [Silence] gives things something of its own holy uselessness."[8]

One of my patients, a forty-eight-year-old man with a deeply troubled past, became more and more beatific as his death from cancer became more imminent. He spent many hours alone, wandering around the city and studying the faces of people out on the streets. He told me:

> I know it sounds crazy, but I feel like I'm ninety years old already. I feel different from everyone I see. It's like I'm not really there any more. Not like they are. Things that matter to them don't matter to me. I see things they don't see. It's wild when you're not in a hurry and everyone else is rushing past you and you know they're not really getting anywhere, because sooner or later all of them will be standing where you are—at the end. You see it and they don't see it.

This man tried to exhort others into his level of awareness, but found that he was unable to induce them away from the concerns to which they were attached. Words alone cannot instigate such breakthroughs.

As a therapist, I move within the limitations of words. Dire events are my allies, because they hasten the process of discovery more than all the reasoning and analysis I can muster. The richest sessions occur when my patients are going through the emptiness that precedes significant change.

Until illness persuades us that time is running out, we may employ a variety of justifications for putting off what we "really" want to do. Remaining for years in a stifling job or hiding in bitterness from intimate relationships are ver-sions of oblivion as potent as many addictions. Gradually, our expended years become so numerous that we can no longer excuse them as a prelude to the "real" content of our lives.

Physical deterioration finally compels us to confront the difference between the life we had hoped to live and the way we are actually living. We can no longer reassure ourselves that "someday" we will accomplish what we have been deferring. While enduring the agony of a kidney stone, Montaigne wrote: "I have at least this profit from the stone, that it will complete what I have still not been able to accomplish in myself and reconcile and familiarize me completely with death."[9] A woman who gave up drinking at age sixty-one explains:

> The worst part about it is all the wasted time. No one can give back to me all the days of my life I spent boozed out of my mind. You can't imagine the regret I feel. Why did I have to wait until my liver gave out? But I tell myself, "At least you didn't go to your grave drunk the way so many do." I'm grateful for every clear-headed day I have to be alive. That's why I go to those AA meetings—I want the young ones there to get smart sooner than I did.

By imposing limits firmer than any we could have previously believed, illness accelerates our ventures into neglected aspects of ourselves. Instead of ruminating over lost opportunities, our task at such times is to recognize what we can still attain and which parts of ourselves can still be salvaged. At the age of sixty-eight, while dying of cancer of the esophagus, the photographer Dorothea Lange told a friend, "It's not so bad knowing you're going to die. It's been a very interesting time since I got the news."

I once sat at the bedside of a thirty-eight-year-old colleague in a cardiac intensive care unit. Stress from overwork had caused his heart to begin beating erratically, to the point that doctors told him he had to change his lifestyle or risk a fatal heart attack. He talked with me all afternoon while we watched his heart beating on the monitor beside his bed. As the hours passed, bursts of thoughts and feelings alternated with long silences. He told me:

The last twenty years seems like someone else's life. It's all so unreal. I can't believe that I put my job before my family, my friends, my health—everything. All I thought about was making money. I'm so lucky that this happened to me and that I didn't die. Now, everything I took for granted seems so precious. When my wife and daughters come to visit, I start crying as soon as I see them.

Realizations that take years to achieve in psychotherapy can happen in hours in a hospital bed. In *Existential Psychotherapy,* Irvin Yalom depicts numerous cases in which his patients were catalyzed by a confrontation with death into "a rapid change in life perspective and a realignment of life's priorities."[10] During times of exigency, change becomes a matter of life and death.

CONVERSIONS

In situations of dependence, there is only one kind of success: the ability to draw others to us rather than drive them away. Up until times of illness, we can define success in a multitude of ways and can pursue it by any means we choose. But dependency has its own rules of conduct and its own route to mastery. Under the pressure of this necessity, many people change more deeply than ever before in their lives.

One sixty-seven-year-old bedbound woman's authoritarian style was so hurtful that she wore out the good will of each of the aides sent to her by a home health care agency. When none of the younger aides would agree to go to her home, an aide with over twenty years of experience decided to go out and make one last try:

I figured I might as well lay it on the line. I said, "Look, lady, no one wants to work for you. You hurt people's feelings. You never say thank you. You order people around. You act like everyone's your servant, not like they're human beings. You try to make people do things they don't want to do. You'd better wise up fast, or all the money in the world won't keep you out of a nursing home." She started crying, saying she didn't realize she was so awful. She thanked me for being honest with her. I couldn't believe it. Her voice got real quiet. I felt bad for her, so I said I would work for her if she was ready to start treating people right. She brightened up and said, yes, she was ready. After that, she was putty in my hands. A real sweet side of her came out, to the point where I actually got to like her.

Our personality styles are not as frozen as we might think. This woman dropped her hard facade when she found that she had pushed her situation to the limit and was left with no other means of fending off abandonment, her worst dread. Treating her helpers with courtesy and respect first served as a lifeline and later struck her as a revelation.

Our faults tend to get worse before they can get better. In *Reclaimed Powers,* David Gutmann points out that if self-centered people do not change as they get older, "the result is an increasing sense of vulnerability that transforms the 'normal' losses and changes of aging into insults, outrages, and terrors."[11] Through the ravages of dependency, many emerge transformed because they have no other choice. They reach the point where they are both appalled by themselves and afraid that they will be left alone.

The psychologist William James examined the written testimonies of those claiming to have undergone religious conversions, seeking clues as to the source of such deep transformations. He noted a similar exhaustion of options and an attitude of surrender preceding the revelations in many of these accounts. He writes:

> There are only two ways in which it is possible to get rid of anger, worry, fear, despair, or other undesirable affections. One is that an opposite affection should overpoweringly break over us, and the other is by getting so exhausted with the struggle that we have to stop,—so we drop down, give up, and *don't care* any longer.[12]

Out of this emptiness, James argues, we derive a readiness for the arrival of a new self. He concludes, "In a large proportion, perhaps the majority, of reports, the writers speak as if the exhaustion of the lower and the entrance of the higher emotion were simultaneous."[13]

A physician tells the story of a man who "hardly did anything but pour out all his grievances, endlessly repeated." Week after week, he took care of this man's medical problems and listened to his complaints. One day, a change occurred:

> Spontaneously, without anything I had said prompting him, he entered upon a confession. He began to talk to me not about the injustices of which he had been a victim, but of the things for which he blamed himself. . . . I was overwhelmed. An immense tenderness invaded my heart. He, too, was visibly transformed, his crabbed features were gradually unbending, lighting up, becoming beautiful. I do not claim that all was changed at once in him, but after that our conversations were quite different.[14]

Conversions are accelerated by conversations, a combination of speaking and being heard, expression and reception. The physician in this instance said very little, but without his presence and tender response this man would not have known what it is to be perceived as beautiful. Whether through prayer or a human-to-human exchange, we turn painful discoveries into new growth when our efforts are witnessed and appreciated, rather than expended in isolation.

Most unsettled by dependency are those who have spent their adulthood shunning close relationships. Illness mandates contact with others, often in physically intimate ways and with a frequency that permits little concealment. When such people are forced to depend on others for their survival, they are thrust into the very aspect of life that once brought them their greatest hurt and disappointment.

By revisiting early sources of pain, we finally allow for their revision. In *What Should Life Mean to You,* Alfred Adler claims that overwhelmingly negative attitudes toward other people and toward life "can be corrected only by reconsidering the situation in which the faulty interpretation was made." He also insists that people generally do not attempt this kind of reexamination "without some social pressure" or without finding that they have no other options.[15]

After undergoing heart surgery, a seventy-nine-year-old man returned home with new ideas about how to conduct his life:

Before, I never even noticed that the lady down the hall had trouble carrying her laundry. Now, when I hear her out there lugging her basket, I rush out and give her a hand. The first time I did it, you should have seen her face. She was shocked. I guess I had the reputation for being a grumpy, selfish old man. I never did do anything for anybody. But being sick like I was woke me up. I hated being so weak. I got so I couldn't lift a grocery bag without getting chest pain. I'm strong again now, but I can't forget how it was. I watch out for people. I figure I'm one of the lucky ones, and I sure better spread it around. I might really need these people someday. And you should see how the ladies in the building bring me pies and kid around with me in the elevator. It's a new life for me now, that's all I can say.

This man was jolted by his illness into discovering that a world of needs existed in addition to his own. Many people cannot give credence to the needs and sufferings of others until they have been helpless themselves. In his treatise on moral behavior, the German philosopher Immanuel Kant proposes that those who are "cold and indifferent to the sufferings of others" may nevertheless learn that it is in their best interests to be of assistance to others, if only because they realize that someday they may need such help themselves.[16]

A fifty-two-year-old man paralyzed by a tumor on his spine claims that he experienced a "conversion phenomenon" after surgery restored partial function to his legs. He writes:

> The shell of protection that I had built around my emotions melted, and my defenses—a wall built of humor, acerbity, and cynicism—fell before a welling of emotion that was a total departure from my usual state of mind. . . . It seemed that the sharp edges of myself had become porous and weak. People could reach into me more easily, and they, in turn, were more vulnerable to me. I did not set hard borders around my identity; I was suffused with a kind of peacefulness, almost a sense of joy. It was all very strange.[17]

After losing both of his parents at a young age, this man suppressed his own needs in order to devote himself to caring for his younger siblings. He then maintained this self-containment long into his adult life. It was not until this vulnerable moment so many years later that he allowed other people take care of him and see into him.

Exposing vulnerability is a reflexive process: the more of ourselves we reveal to others, the more others tend to reveal of themselves. One sixty-two-year-old man became so desperate in reaction to his failing health that he finally did something out of character: he brought together a group of male friends who were in the same predicament and revealed his struggles to them. He recalls what he realized at that time:

> All my life I had been forced to focus on externals; to focus on anything else was regarded as idle daydreaming. But the externals, when applied to the stretch of life that now lay ahead of me—aging, old age, a probable terminal illness, death and a possible world beyond—left me absolutely nothing. . . . The inner landscape, once it was really discovered and lived in, was aglow.[18]

With this man's leadership, the men began discussing concerns they had never verbalized during their active business careers: feelings of vulnerability and fear, and questions about the value of what they had done with their lives. Gradually, this group grew into a club dedicated to helping others make the shift from external to internal reverence.

YIELDING

The chance to explore unlived life awaits us as long as we are alive, but only if we are willing to succumb to radical change. In *Centering: In Pottery, Poetry, and the Person*, M. C. Richards notes, "To yield means both to lose and to gain. . . . I yield, and my being increases and takes form by having been given up in this way."[19] In many respects, we have to die to the life we previously led in order to open ourselves to the discoveries that incite growth of this nature.

A woman in her early sixties realized one day that she would never be able to run again. Bone loss in her legs had been causing her pain, even when walking. She writes:

> I grieve with this new knowledge and realize that I cannot remember when I last ran. What I am always aware of, somewhere in the back of my mind but not taken out and examined as I do now on this page, is that I am in the process of dying and that all of this is a part of the life experience. One doesn't just die all of a sudden. It is a process and one we may be conscious of for the last ten or twenty years of our life, which if you think about it, may be a quarter or more of your lifetime. I find myself wondering why this is not more talked about and why it has not become the common knowledge of our lives.[20]

Long before we dare to speak the words, we receive reminders that we are in a slow process of dying. A pain that will not cease or an injury that will not heal announces the arrival of limitations we have always feared. From the beginning, we know that our capacities are temporary, yet it startles us once we actually start losing them.

A psychiatrist cites several cases in which older men sought psychotherapy because of impotency, noting that "loss of sexual potency was frequently equated by all of these men with the end of their lives, as if sexuality was the central force governing their lives and lending it any and all color and purpose." One man told him:

> I used to ski deep powder all day long, but I can't do it anymore. My thighs begin to quiver after about an

> hour of it, and I have to stop. It's the same thing as sex,
> I can't go on as long there, too, as I used to. It's not a
> good feeling. It makes me feel older and used up. I
> don't like it.[21]

It is dangerous to locate our identity in quarters as vulnerable as the body. The occurrence of an incurable illness
or an untreatable injury immediately reveals how far we
have erred in this direction. In "Psychological Developments in the Second Half of Life," Robert Peck writes,
"Some people cling to physical powers, both as their chief
'tool' for coping with life, and as the most important ele-
ment in . . . their self-definition. Since physical powers inev-
itably decline, such people tend to grow increasingly depressed, bitter, or otherwise unhappy as they grow older."[22]

Just as perilous as using physical powers for one's self-
definition is relying upon one's occupational status. A seventy-nine-year-old man who led an active professional life
up until retirement explains, "Old age for me has been the
recognition of what was left when all that I was was taken
away from me."[23] A man who retired from an influential ad-
ministrative post in a university told me:

> The phone doesn't ring any more. You realize that
> people had been calling for the title and the position,
> not the person. Once the title's gone, they have no use
> for you. You're not there at work, and they don't go
> out of their way to see you. Sure, some are happy to
> run into you socially, but the thing is, you don't matter
> any more. It's a hard adjustment.

During times of illness, both occupations and physical
pleasures fall away in one avalanche of loss. We are left with
life in its most reduced state. In *Suicide and the Soul*, James

Hillman suggests, "When illusions are worked through, what remains is often smaller than what was hoped, because becoming oneself means being reduced to just what one is—that stone of common clay."[24]

Far from the ordeal many imagine it to remain, this situation of depletion often evolves into a period of uncanny contentment. Feeling they have little left to lose, some people gradually become more daring than ever before in their lives. The more they relinquish of their former identity, the freer they feel about trying out parts of themselves that have lain fallow for years. A seventy-year-old man explains, "I will say things now that I wouldn't have done twenty years ago, although they were in my mouth. But now I don't care. I was shy, very shy, as a younger man, but now I speak."[25]

Speaking at last without pretense or caution bestows a power toward which other people respond. In "The Moment of Truth: Care of the Dying Person," Cicely Saunders notes, "People who are dying often have a tremendous capacity for meeting, or encountering, because they have put aside the mask that we tend to wear in everyday life. Now they are ready to meet, just as themselves, and I am sure this is why you can get to know these patients in an extraordinarily short time."[26]

In the film "Ikiru," Akira Kurosawa portrays the story of a man who receives a fatal diagnosis of cancer and is unable to continue on with his twenty-five-year career as a civil servant. He goes out in search of the life he deferred. In a bar, he meets a writer who is struck by his situation. The writer tells him:

> You've made me really think tonight. I see that adversity has its virtues—man finds truth in misfortune; having cancer has made you want to taste life. Man is such

a fool. It is always just when he is going to leave it that he discovers how beautiful life can be. And even then, people who realize this are rare. Some die without ever once knowing what life is really like. You're a fine man, you're fighting against death—that's what impresses me. Up until now you've been life's slave but now you're going to be its master.[27]

Yielding and mastery are two sides of the same command over life. While we are still able-bodied, we tend to feel cheated when mishaps interfere with our strivings. Physical incapacity reverses this stance: we expect our desires to be frustrated, and we are relieved when small portions of our preferences are satisfied. The philosopher Arthur Schopenhauer observes, "In youth, a man fancies that there is a prodigious amount of happiness and pleasure to be had in the world, only that it is difficult to come by it; whereas, when he becomes old, he knows that there is nothing of the kind; he makes his mind completely at ease on the matter."[28]

To varying degrees, unlived life is everyone's plight. Our time is finite, our abilities are uneven, and we have to forsake some goals in order to attain others. These limitations are there all along, but illness finally forces us to reconcile ourselves to them. A man diagnosed with cancer told his physician, "I always imagined I'd do something great. I'm sure I have it in me. . . . But now I may not have the time. I feel like it's all gone. I am who I am, no more and no less."[29] Also facing a diagnosis of cancer, a fifty-nine-year-old woman wrote in her journal:

> You feel a loss of options. The Greek you were going to study someday, the lover you might take, the house you would have by the sea, the children whose children

you looked forward to, the finally successful, definitive book you were going to write—it was all fantasy maybe (or maybe not), and any and all might still happen; but everything seems less likely. Life is no longer open-ended.[30]

Accepting death, the final disruption of our plans, is the yielding that brings us closest to something like happiness. We realize that we are not, and have never been, in control of our lives in the way we may have desired. In *Reveries of the Solitary Walker,* Jean-Jacques Rousseau claims, "I have seen few if any happy people." Instead, he explains, there is a kind of contentment which arises once we accede to the constancy of change. He writes:

Everything here on earth is in a continual flux which allows nothing to assume any constant form. All things change round about us, we ourselves change, and no one can be sure of loving tomorrow what he loves today. All our plans for happiness in this life are therefore empty dreams. Let us make the most of peace of mind when it comes to us, taking care to do nothing to drive it away, but not making plans to hold it fast, since such plans are sheer folly.[31]

§

To fulfill our promises to ourselves is to prepare to die; tragedy is to die with unlived life still inside us. In *Heading Home,* Senator Paul Tsongas recounts his decision to end his political career in response to getting cancer. He quotes a comment written to him by a friend: "No one on his deathbed ever said, 'I wish I had spent more time on my business.' "[32]

When he turned forty, Rousseau vowed to himself "to

order my inner life for the rest of my days as I would wish it to be at the time of my death." He then resigned a lucrative government post and took up work "copying music at so much a page," an occupation which had always given him pleasure and which allowed him time for reading and writing, the activities he most valued.[33]

SEVEN

Refusing to Be Demeaned

A sixty-six-year-old woman with degenerative arthritis decided to give up leaving her apartment entirely, rather than go on enduring an outside world which spurned her:

> I walk funny, I know I do. But up here, in my own place, my legs don't matter. There's nothing I can't do for myself. Anyone who comes in and sits at my table is my equal. Out on the street, I'm a crippled old lady, a nothing. You should see how people look away from me. And the drivers. If I don't make it across the street before the light changes, forget it. Some of them honk and yell curses at me. I've made up my mind: here I'm safe and secure. I've got plenty to read and plenty to think about. If I really want to see what's going on out there, I can look out my window.

People impeded by either illness or frailty often feel demeaned by the world around them. Rejections come at them from all directions, from random strangers to providers of medical care. A man confined to a wheelchair observes, "The disabled serve as constant visible reminders to

111

the able-bodied that the society they live in is shot through with inequity and suffering, and that they live in a counterfeit paradise."[1]

Dignity is a solitary attribute. Other people can detract from it, but we have to replenish it on our own. In situations of physical incapacity, self-possession is maintained by literally holding onto oneself in spite of every possible infringement. A man disabled in a car accident claims, "I soon learned that it was considered bad form for me to behave like a normal person in certain situations."[2]

This chapter examines these hurtful reactions and the difficult feat of improvising self-respect in the midst of them. Medical situations are examined first, since ill and disabled people usually cannot avoid these encounters. Social situations are then dissected to reveal their potential for both the demise and assertion of dignity. Finally, the components of self-respect are appraised on the personal plane, where both care and harm from others is most intimately rendered.

MEDICAL CONTEMPT

An eighty-four-year-old woman describes a ten-minute encounter with her doctor:

> I even made a list, so I could remember what to ask him. I wanted to know why my legs get quivery on my front steps. You know, it's not like me to stay home all the time. When the doctor came in, right away he started asking me about my medicines. He wanted to know about this and that. Before I knew it, he had to go. The nurse was there, saying he had to go see someone else. He told me about my new prescriptions and

said to come see him in a month. I was so frustrated, I
could have screamed.

Medical contempt hurts as much as any illness. Amidst pressures to hurry, patients who slow things down are regarded
as obstacles. Those who cannot hear or see well, or who ask
that information be repeated, or who need to discuss their
problems thoroughly are especially dreaded by hurried
staff.

In the last few decades, large corporations have been
purchasing hospitals, nursing homes, and clinics. The result is that health care is being transformed from a public
service to a private business. In *The Social Transformation of
American Medicine,* Paul Starr writes: "The rise of the for-
profit chains has, for the first time, introduced managerial
capitalism into American medicine on a large scale."[3] These
facilities are in business to make money, and whatever ob-
structs that purpose is strategically dispensed or elimi-
nated.

Health care is the most crucial product that we pur-
chase, but we do so when we are least able either to insist on
what we need or to ensure that what we get is of good quality. It is estimated that more than eighty percent of the
money we spend on health care in our lifetimes is spent in
the last few months of life, when we are likely to be captive
and helpless.[4] Robert Miner, a hospital orderly, offers his
observations:

> The sad truth about modern medicine is that people
> who work with patients don't have time. . . . [For exam-
> ple] the old man retching on a stretcher in the hall out-
> side X-ray, begging to be transported back to his room
> where he could at least suffer in private: I had prom-
> ised X-ray I'd come for him as soon as I moved medica-
> tion to the intensive care unit. Meanwhile there were

surgical instruments waiting to go to the operating
room, an intravenous machine they needed in pediat-
rics. . . . They are short-handed everywhere in hospitals
and the excuse is that modern medicine costs too
much to hire more staff.[5]

This "old man retching on a stretcher in the hall" was
caught by one of the details of hospital care that matter the
most: how long we are kept waiting when we are suffering.
News reports about staff shortages in hospitals do not make
the implications vivid enough for the public outcry they de-
serve.

Until we are actually receiving medical services, we
have few ways to judge the quality of one facility over another beyond what we can see with our eyes. Plush waiting
rooms and much-heralded advances in technology seem to
assure us that medical excellence will be there when we
need it. We cannot see that technology has become more
profitable to implement than the more fundamental aspects of mercy.

Hospitals once made mercy their chief objective. In
The Care of Strangers, Charles Rosenberg explains that hospitals were originally almshouses where the poor could go to
receive care and shelter during illness and old age. Only
people without family support came to these early hospitals, which were staffed by nuns and other members of religious orders. The staff usually resided at the facility and
stayed on for years. There was little privacy among the rows
of beds in the wards and minimal technology practiced by
the staff, but the care was generally personal and compassionate. Rosenberg writes:

The modern hospital's basic shape had been established by 1920. It had become central to medical education and was well integrated into the career patterns

of regular physicians; in urban areas it had already re-
placed the family as the site for treating serious illness
and managing death. Perhaps most important, it had
already been clothed with a legitimating aura of sci-
ence and almost boundless social expectation.[6]

From almshouses to medical training to money-making
ventures represents an immense shift in mission and style
of management. Many of today's for-profit hospital and
clinic chains offer staff a salary bonus for taking care of
more than their quota of patients per day. In such settings,
it is not in a doctor or nurse's best interests to linger, listen,
or desist from using expensive equipment. On the contrary,
listening at length to patients' concerns can ruin a staff
member's productivity score and result in censure from em-
ployers.

Listening and explaining, no matter how time-
consuming and therefore costly, remain important to patients as they face difficult choices. A ninety-two-year-old
woman once grabbed my hand while I was rushing by her
hospital bed. She begged me to listen to her, even though I
was not the social worker assigned to her case:

> Please, please, get these doctors to listen to me.
> They're sending me downstairs any minute to stick
> tubes in me, to see where I'm bleeding. I don't care
> where I'm bleeding. Why doesn't anyone listen? I'm
> ready to die. I've had a good life. Now I just want to lie
> here, in peace. Please, can you make them understand?
> They keep coming in here and patting me on the arm
> and telling me it will be all right, but they don't cancel
> the test. Maybe they'll listen to you, a nice young lady,
> if you tell them for me.

An expert on chronic illness claims that people with
intractable physical problems yearn to talk with their doc-

tors. Above all, he insists, they want their doctors to see more of them than is immediately apparent in a hospital bed or exam room. He writes, "Illness story making and telling are particularly prevalent among the elderly . . . so for the care giver what is important is to witness a life story, to validate its interpretation, and to affirm its value."[7]

When someone is frightened or in pain, speaking up to this extent is not easy. If a physician talks quickly and uses obscure language, the person is doubly silenced. In *Psychological Care in Physical Illness,* Keith Nichols bemoans the "inflexible questioning pattern" used by many physicians. He found in his research that such patterns frequently prevent patients from bringing up their own concerns.[8]

One strategy patients often use successfully is to write down their questions before seeing the doctor. They then hand over this list when the doctor appears. In this way, patients do not have to struggle to find the right words or to recall questions that were nagging at them earlier. Patients thereby set the agenda for the discussion, not the physician.

Still more important than lists is understanding the implications of the changes that have occurred in mission and staff compensation. We can no longer assume that physicians are our agents, resolutely looking out for our best interests. A philosopher of medical ethics asserts, "Patients will not trust providers who put their own economic gain above patient needs. They will be especially distrustful of schemes that allow doctors to profit by denying care."[9]

When time-management techniques belonging to factories are applied to health care settings, patients feel efficiently processed rather than humanely served. Tasks are given priority over feelings, productivity over kindness. No matter how cleverly the owners of for-profit facilities measure the caliber of care they provide, medical contempt remains more profitable than mercy.

Maggie Kuhn, founder of the Gray Panthers, offers her personal observations about the effects of such changes in the practice of health care:

> My brother died after being hospitalized for three months in three hospitals. . . . I was depressed and enraged by the way in which the whole health care system has been specialized. There was a succession of six different nurses who saw him. Each spent a few seconds—a couple of minutes at the most—but nobody looked at him as a whole person. . . . It was the nurse's aides who had more continuous contact with him and who saw to it that he was looked after. How accurate can the reports be when each primary nurse is responsible for an incredible number of patients, with very little time to spend with each?[10]

VITAL DEFIANCE

Medical settings tend to be microcosms of the societies that sustain them. Upon returning home from a trip to the Middle East, a woman with multiple sclerosis realized that in America, by contrast, "there is much less tolerance for incompetence or inefficiency." She suddenly saw the values underlying American intolerance in sharp relief: that self-sufficiency is virtuous, that outcomes must be controllable, that doing is better than being, and that the future is more valuable than the past. She writes:

> I have no control over the disease activity in my brain. In and of itself, this is hard enough to accept, but acceptance does come. That acceptance is infinitely harder to achieve, however, when the culture continually—in both small and big ways—tells me I should be in control, that control is possible . . . I hear constantly

that acceptance is passive and weak; to rage and fight would be much more acceptable . . . If, finally, I manage to accept that I am not independent—responsible for myself, yes, but clearly unable to live autonomously—then I live at odds with the dominant thrust of my culture.[11]

People whose physical powers are constricted cannot live by American values, which presume that one is able-bodied and independent. Those who are not self-sufficient cannot control the outcomes of ordinary tasks, let alone their larger undertakings. They dare not invest their self-esteem solely in what they are able to accomplish, and they cannot afford to live for a future that may be more difficult than their present or past. Their strength resides in evolving an individual set of values that bolsters the kind of life they are able to live, rather than the life that others live. A woman disabled by polio as a child explains, "I understood that it was up to me to establish my own system to live by."[12]

Older people who have retained their good health and full physical capacities often find themselves similarly estranged. By virtue of age, most no longer go along with our culture's preference for the future over the past, and retirement may have hurtled them into days more focused on being than doing. Watching their peers cope with physical problems, they may regard their self-sufficiency as a perishable privilege. In addition to these pressures, everywhere they look aging itself is scorned. A woman in the midst of this struggle writes:

Old is ugly, old is powerless, old is the end, and therefore . . . old is what no one could possibly want to be. At sixty-nine, I take in these messages from the outside every day, and I have had to learn ways of reacting to all the negative messages around me in order to survive. . . . In a day of living as an old woman, I reach for all the ways possible on that particular day, in that given moment. . . . Proving that I'm still strong, capable, sexual, is a response I give to a negative world a dozen times a day.[13]

Deflecting disdain on so many levels at once takes considerable stamina. Instead, many older people absorb the contempt and begin to despise themselves for no longer being young. They shrink themselves down to the size of these degrading expectations, taking on an outer demeanor which constrains their self-expression but which is regarded by others as more acceptable for their age.

Older or disabled people who insist on remaining themselves face an exhausting divergence between who they know themselves to be and how others treat them. They feel drained each time strangers respond to them in terms of the category "old" or "disabled." In *The Coming of Age*, Simone de Beauvoir deplores the gap she feels at the age of sixty between her inner sense of herself and how strangers react to her as an older woman. She points out, "Old age is particularly difficult to assume because we have always regarded it as something alien, a foreign species: 'Can I have become a different being while I still remain myself?' "[14]

Destructive reactions, such as the tendency to equate old age or disability with mental deficiency, are surprisingly common. In *A Good Age*, Alex Comfort tells the story of a well-intentioned young senator who gave a group of older people a tour around the Senate Chamber:

He treated them a little like schoolchildren; explaining the legislative process in words of one syllable and shouting in case they were deaf. Finally, turning to one of the group, the Senator asked, "And what used you to be?" The old man fixed a beady eye on him and replied, "I still am."[15]

Self-preservation can sometimes be accomplished in a sentence. Usually, however, the struggle is more protracted and the feelings that are aroused cannot be handled so succinctly. Repeatedly treated as simple-minded, many people begin to question their intelligence and competence. So little regard reaches older and disabled people from the outside world that their inner stores of confidence may slowly become depleted. In *The Unexpected Minority,* John Gliedman and William Roth assert, "Far more is involved than what occurs at the given moment of an encounter. . . . Handicapped individuals meet the able-bodied every day. . . . It is a history of *learned* inferiority."[16]

Aged and disabled people must constantly find ways to override other people's inability to see them. Being seen is fundamental to being respected. A man who learned how to project his distinctiveness despite others' preconceived reactions to his wheelchair observes, "You know after talking with someone for awhile when they don't see the handicap any more. That's when you've broken through."[17]

The labor of breaking through almost always rests with the stigmatized person. In "Deviance Disavowal: The Management of Strained Interaction By the Visibly Handicapped," Fred Davis explains that in this effort "the handicapped person projects images, attitudes and concepts of self" to encourage able-bodied people to be at ease and carry on with the conversation in normal ways."[18] Such assertion is an indispensable form of defiance.

A man in his seventies told me what happened when he attended a concert given by a popular rock group:

I was standing on line to get a good seat. A kid in front of me turned around and saw my white hair and white beard. "What are *you* doing here?" he asked, as if I was from outer space. I said, "The same thing you're doing. Trying to get into this concert." I stared him right in the eye. He said, "O.K, man," like it suddenly dawned on him that maybe an old man can like rock music, too. It hurt. I didn't have a good time after that. I've been going to concerts for years, and no one ever said that before. I felt like I didn't belong there any more.

At first, this man succumbed to the rejection. He stopped going to concerts and taking his customary walks and bus rides all over town. He started referring to himself as "an old man" and lost the spring in his step. Finally, however, it occurred to him that for every person who made a snide remark or gave him a contemptuous glance there would surely be others who would derive hope for their own future from his presence there. Once he resumed his concert-going, his depression resolved.

Acts of self-assertion do not have to be monumental to be vitalizing. In a nursing home where I worked for a year, one ninety-eight-year-old resident became furious each time aides tried to change her incontinent pad later than 2:00 P.M. She would scold them vehemently, claiming that they were making her late for the 3:00 coffee hour. Since they usually completed their task by 2:30, the aides considered her rage to be both abusive and unreasonable. One day, by chance, I happened to be sitting in the lounge at 2:30. This woman approached me in her wheelchair, asking me if I would be kind enough to move to another table. She explained:

This is the only table that's the right height for resting your coffee cup, to be able to sip it without having to pick it up. You see, my hands have a terrible tremor, so otherwise I'd get coffee all over my dress. You have to get here early or you don't get this table. With my hands being so bad, I've got to leave my room by 2:15 at the latest or I don't get here on time. Just a few inches is all I get out of each push on these wheels. There's no way I can get here any faster.

This woman held fiercely to her remaining capacities. She was dependent on staff for assistance in getting dressed in the morning and undressed at night, as well as for getting in and out of the bathroom, but she needed no one to feed her or push her wheelchair. For each of us, there is a limit to the amount of surrender we are able to countenance without losing ourselves.

CONTRADICTIONS

Ill and disabled people often become caught in perplexing contradictions. A man bedbound with cancer explains:

There I was home in bed, just a terrible burden to everyone. But at the same time I resented them for going on with their lives. I didn't want them to bother, I really wanted to be alone most of the time anyway, but I still wanted them to take care of me. Isn't that crazy?[19]

Wanting both to be assisted and to be left alone, to be accommodated and to live normally, dependent people may push help away at the same time that they hope others will find ways to make life easier for them. A woman coping with a debilitating illness in her late thirties admits, "I do not wish to be treated as though I am sick. However, I find that I would like people to quietly notice and make allowances."[20] A man dependent on his wife's assistance with getting dressed, eating, and turning over in bed at night attests to a "powerful pull backward into the self . . . [that] becomes compelling, often irresistable."[21]

In *Listening with the Third Ear,* the analyst Theodor Reik points out that such dividedness is not a problem to be solved, but rather an aspect of the human condition that must be accepted:

> Opposite tendencies can coexist in us, feelings contradicting each other live together, and what is true and what false can be confused. . . . So much lives in us—wishes and their denials, faith and mistrust, appetites and distastes. They change places so frequently that what is fair becomes foul and what is foul, fair.[22]

The more independence we lose, the more torn we become by contradictory urges. Outbursts of anger at helpers who are only doing what is necessary is one of the indisputable signs of this turmoil. When success at even ordinary tasks becomes elusive, some people resent being rescued as much as they want desperately to be spared their frustrations. A fifty-nine-year-old man paralyzed on one side by a stroke explains:

> Getting my shirt on in the morning is a big thing for me. My wife sits there while I fumble. It's hard for me to get the sleeve to line up so my arm gets through the hole. It takes her just a second to help me, but if she does I yell at her. And when she doesn't, I resent the hell out of her. How's that for a setup? There's no way for either of us to win.

To accept help is to miss a chance to prevail, and to go on struggling is taxing and upsetting. A woman with rheumatoid arthritis writes, "The moments I still feel raw anger are those when I battle unforgiving mechanical objects— . . . squeezing a gas pump handle, fighting a screw that won't budge. Those things remind me of helplessness and they raise a rage. I hate asking for help."[23]

Asking for help is more complicated than it seems, often evoking a host of conflicted emotions. Some dependent people find the mere act of calling attention to themselves abhorrent. Others can bear this indignity but dislike having to spell out exactly what has to be done on their behalf. Almost all tire of explaining, revealing, and excusing themselves, wishing that people would know what to do and would simply do it without having to be asked or reminded. An eighty-three-year-old woman who was forced to give up driving due to a stroke explains:

> Every Sunday I need a ride to church. But when I call somebody, I can never tell how they really feel about going out of their way to get me. Some people say "yes" when they mean "no." I can feel it later on, when I get into the car. They sort of let me know how much traffic there was, or how much earlier they had to leave the house—that kind of thing. It would be so much easier all around if people would just offer once in a while, when they really feel they can spare the time. Asking is a horrible position, for them and for me.

The best assistance is that which is unobtrusive. Helpers who quietly get things done, rather than announcing their efforts, leave a dependent person's pride intact. The indebted position is not emphasized, and no mention is made of special accommodations. The fact of helplessness then recedes into the background, where it can reside without harming the person's self-esteem.

The conflict between asking for help and preserving

one's dignity is most intense around the functions of elimi-
nation. Once these functions become impaired, they move
from the domain of unconcern to utter domination. Worrying about staining a friend's upholstered couch, or having
to be constantly aware of the location of the nearest toilet
are concerns that are demeaning by their very intrusive-
ness. Yet letting others in on these worries may not yield
enough support to be worth the embarrassment. In *Stigma:
Notes on the Management of Spoiled Identity,* Erving Goffman
marvels at the relentless dilemmas of "information control" faced by disabled people: "To display or not to display; to tell or not to tell; to let on or not to let on; to lie or
not to lie; and in each case, to whom, how, when, and
where."[24]

A thirty-eight-year-old man with a bowel ailment depicts the large difference that true support can make:

> Sometimes I need the bathroom in a hurry. I just don't
> get the warning other people get. So I like to be places
> where there's more than one bathroom and where
> people automatically reserve the closest one for me.
> I've got cousins who always use their downstairs bath-
> room whenever I come over, and they don't say a word
> about it—they just do it. I relax at their house like no-
> where else, because I don't have to worry and I don't
> even have to ask.

Repeatedly needing to ask for rides, favors, and special
adaptations causes many ill and disabled people to feel they
must ask for nothing on other levels. Some try to compensate by extending themselves in every other way, such as becoming good listeners who rarely expect others to listen in
return. One woman with a disability explains, "I think because of being aware of my particular physical needs and
having to ask for concessions and help, I don't ask emotion-

ally. I compensate by being the Rock of Gibraltar in the emotional department."[25]

Concealment, whether physical or emotional, only produces a lonely form of dignity. A woman in her early sixties found that hiding the downturns in her illness from her daughter left both of them isolated. She writes, "I am torn between a fear of imposing on her, mother leaning too heavily on daughter (as mine did on me), and her obvious desire to have only truth from me."[26] Separating oneself from sources of comfort and nurturance becomes too steep a sacrifice for pride.

Others go the opposite way and cede their independence entirely, finding that it is easier to give up all personal power than to remain conflicted about retaining it. They cease voicing their preferences, eventually losing their zest for living as a result of their capitulation. Those ministering to such people often long for some show of resistance, or at least for the chance to respond to a clear request. A woman caring for her eighty-year-old mother-in-law observes:

> If some parents become cantankerous, she's become withdrawn, fearful of asking for anything. I'm unsettled by her selflessness. . . . Now she seems like an empty shell. Although she has the love and respect of her children, which is more than most of us have these days, I don't want to end up like that.[27]

The exercise of influence is essential to retaining both vibrancy and self-respect. Unless we exert control over some aspect of our lives, no matter how mundane or seemingly inconsequential, a significant part of our spirit dies. In his autobiography about his years in slavery, Frederick Douglass describes an incident in which he physically resisted one of his masters, stating, "It recalled to life my crushed self-respect, and my self-confidence.... Human nature is so constituted, that it cannot honor a helpless man, though it can pity him, and even this it cannot do long if signs of power do not arise."[28]

In situations of dependence, power can be reclaimed through may routes. Any strategy that lessens ambiguity restores authority to dependent people. Insisting that their helpers function according to a schedule is better for their endurance than putting up with long hours of waiting. Just as waiting reminds them minute-by-minute of their helplessness, firm plans convey a semblance of their former control over their lives. When dependent people can count on events taking place at a set time, they can anticipate them almost as if autonomy were still in their possession. There is no waiting, no asking, and no infuriating uncertainty.

Other ways of taking back control may be more subtle but just as beneficial. A sixty-eight-year-old homebound woman describes her system for managing the benevolence upon which she depends:

> One of my neighbors is full of religion and she just wants me to listen to that stuff while she makes up my bed. Another one just wants me to notice the special things she gets for me when she does my shopping. And there's one that can't stand it if I thank her, so I have to act like the treats she brings me are the most natural things in the world. Each one's different. I like to give them what they want, so they'll keep being good to me.

This woman survives by remaining attuned to what her helpers expect in return for their kindness. She carefully maintains the exchange, watching to see that each of her helpers leaves satisfied. She derives pride and security

from accurately detecting what each is getting out of helping her and making sure that these rewards continue to sat-
isfy them.

Successfully handling the needs and anxieties of their
helpers frequently becomes a source of strength for dependent people. A disabled man notes how his forthright requests for aid tend to relieve those who are not sure how to
approach him: "Innumerable times I have seen the fear and
bewilderment in people's eyes vanish as I have stretched out
my hand for help, and I have felt life and warmth stream
from the helping hands I have taken."[29]

Until they arrive at compromises that allow for both
self-assertion and collaboration, dependent people are often
drawn back and forth on a confusing pendulum of contradictions. They are never sure how much leaning on others
is acceptable and how much effort they should exert in
their attempts to overcome obstacles and frustrations. A
man disabled in his youth by polio writes, "Asking for help
has always been difficult . . . but hardest of all was to ask for
something that I knew I *could* do. In fact, if I could do it,
there was a moral imperative *to* do it, no matter how tired I
was or what risk it demanded."[30]

§

The English language reduces our situation to terms of
deficiency when we become ill or incapacitated. In *Missing
Pieces: A Chronicle of Living with a Disability,* Irving Zola writes,
"We are de-formed, dis-eased, dis-abled, dis-ordered, ab-
normal and, most telling of all, called an in-valid."[31] These
words depict deviations from the normal, instead of allowing these circumstances their own validity.

A woman confined to her apartment by an inoperable
problem with her hips explains:

I still feel vivacious. I can hardly walk across the room, but I wake up in the morning raring to go. I forget that I'm eighty and that my hips don't work anymore. Sometimes I start getting up off my chair as if I'm really going somewhere and boom, it hits—I remember that I'm a gorgeous dame stuck in a worn-out body. But this is the price I pay to be alive.

EIGHT _____

The Fiction of Independence

There are moments in life when our true dependence on one another breaks through. One woman explains:

> I'm only thirty-five, but getting really sick last winter made me think about what would happen at the end of my life. I started wondering who would take care of me if I couldn't take care of myself. I told a few of my friends that I wanted to move in with them if anything happens to me. The idea of living near my friends is now more important to me than getting the greatest job or going back to school to get the fanciest degree. My illness really changed how I see friendship altogether.

As soon as health problems threaten our autonomy, loyalty becomes the attribute we most value in our relatives and celebrate in our friends. The partner of a man dying of AIDS quotes a remark made to him by a friend: "All that will matter to you when you're old is how much you are loved."[1]

People who have never been seriously ill tend to doubt

such assertions, while amost everyone who has been ill or disabled swears to this wisdom. In "Dying in a Technological Society," Eric Cassell points out that we may try to ignore our connectedness to one another so long as we possess good health, but that in sickness "the fiction of independence and the denial of fate give way to reality."[2]

This chapter examines community, friendship, and generosity, three aspects of life that we may squander until we fully admit to our dependence on one another. No matter what our previous attitudes, illness leaves little doubt that our need for attachment to others persists throughout the lifespan and that it matters more than anything else at the end.

STAYING IN PLACE

If we conducted the middle of our lives with an eye to the end of our lives, we would choose a place to live and we would stay. Residing near others with whom we establish a history of reciprocity is the best hope for old age or disability, whether we manage to live near blood relations or choose to develop family-like bonds with others. A sixty-six-year-old woman explains:

> I've lived in this apartment more than twenty years already. So even when I had to start using this wheelchair, I decided to stay put. There's no point going any place else, even if they have ramps and special bathtubs. I've known my neighbors for years now. Any time I need a quart of milk or a head of lettuce, it seems someone's asking me if I need anything at the store. I did a lot for them, and they haven't forgotten. If I moved someplace new, I couldn't do anything for any-

one. I'd just be a burden. No one would remember me
any other way. I'd rather stay where people know who
I am.

Loyalty is a reward for remembered generosity. Moving to an accessible building would have improved this
woman's immediate independence, but at the sacrifice of
her long-term security. No amount of self-reliance can
match the confidence derived from years of faithfulness
and accumulated gratitude.

To be compelled to leave one's home was once considered a terrible fate. Yet in the modern age, we commonly
forfeit bonds of loyalty in order to improve our circumstances materially. We voluntarily turn ourselves into displaced people. We recognize our displacement as exile
only when the time comes that we need to call on others
for help.

Many people living in rural areas still recognize the
value of interdependence as a way of life. In 1989, I visited
a small town in West Virginia and stayed with a family who
had resided there for several generations. After dinner the
first night, my sixty-two-year-old host excused herself from
the table with this explanation:

I have to go make some phone calls. There's a few
women I call every night between 8:30 and 9:00. They
live alone, and they're in their eighties and nineties. I
like to make sure they're OK. Having someone to talk
to at the end of the day does them a world of good,
even just for a few minutes. They know someone is
thinking of them, and they can say a thing or two about
how their day was. I know they really look forward to
it. The whole business takes me less than a half hour at
the most.

This woman could not have separated herself from the fate of people she had known since her youth. As far back as she could remember, they had been part of the landscape of her life. She had known them long before health problems forced them to withdraw from active roles in the community. Watching over their welfare was more a reflex than an effort.

Our concept of community was once bounded by living in a particular place. In *Community and Social Change in America,* Thomas Bender shows how improved transportation and communication have since made "social networks completely independent of territory." He writes, "In contemporary America, men and women do not so much move from one town to another as follow an advantageous career path that may take them to a number of basically incidental locations."[3]

The problem with our modern networks is that they become useless once physical frailty catapults our mobility back into the nineteenth century. When we can no longer drive or mount the steps of a bus or negotiate busy airports, we have to resort to face-to-face, immediate communities. Where we reside once again determines the nature of the life that we live. An eighty-two-year-old woman explains how drastically one's territory can shrink with the onset of physical difficulties:

> I haven't seen my best friend in five years, and she lives right here in town. Can you imagine that? I can't see well enough to go out alone, and she can't get down her front steps unless someone practically carries her. She can't impose on her family to give her a ride over, because they already do so much for her. There's only three miles between us, but it may as well be three thousand miles. We talk every morning on the phone, but there's nothing like sitting down with someone

and having a cup of coffee. So I've forced myself to get to know some of the women right here in the building.

In a study of elderly urban widows, the sociologist Helena Lopata compared those who had not moved since their bereavement with those who had immediately relocated. She found that those who had stayed in place were "more fully involved in neighboring than any of the movers." She quotes a woman in her seventies who had moved to live with her son but who then returned to her old neighborhood after three months: "From my experience, I think the problem is that you miss your own age group. I am much happier to be with my own friends." Another woman in the study speculates as to why her area contains so many widows: "I think, for one thing, they've lived here for so long that they just stay here because all their friends are here and it's too difficult to start over at an older age."[4]

Prior to reaching our time of frailty, we are wise to survey our lives for pockets of loyalty worth preserving. Starting over is strenuous at any age, but especially when we are emotionally vulnerable or physically fragile. A seventy-year-old woman who moved to be near her son when her health started to fail explains:

I always thought that living near your children was the most important thing—after a certain age. So I said yes right away when my son offered to turn his basement into an apartment for me. At first, I was glad I moved, but I found out that your family can't fill your life. You see them at dinner time but you've got the whole day to fill until then. Plus, you don't really know each other any more. They try to make you feel comfortable, but you feel like an outsider—you have different tastes, different things you like to do, a different way of life. Back home, I always had people around when I wanted them. You know a lot of people when you live somewhere as long as I lived there. I want to move back, but don't know how to tell this to my son. He's been so good to me, and I don't want to hurt him.

Reciprocation keeps relationships alive. Bonds with friends and neighbors may mean more than blood ties, especially if a recent history of giving and receiving animates these other relationships. Such discoveries contradict what we prefer to believe about the strength of family bonds and our ability to overcome the effects of geographical separation. Scattering across the country causes family members to become strangers to each other, no matter how often they write or call. Verbal contact is not the same as meshing the routines of daily life: going shopping together, exchanging help back and forth, and witnessing each other's victories and sorrows first-hand.

When she was seventy-five, the anthropologist Margaret Mead suggested in an interview that "we in America have very little sense of interdependence." She asserted, "The real issue is whether a society keeps its older people close to children and young people. If old people are separated from family life, there is real tragedy both for them and the young."[5] A sixty-year-old woman told me about the day she was summoned out of the periphery of her daughter's life:

She called and said, "Mom, I need your help." I couldn't believe my ears, because she'd always been the independent type. Her husband had left her, and she needed me to come out there right away to give her a hand with the children. I'd been a widow for five years already, so I was used to being on my own. Who wants to take care of young children at my age? It was a big change for me, giving up my freedom, but I went.

It's been good for me and good for them. I'm close to
the kids now, not just a voice on the phone. And I don't
worry so much about the future any more. If I get sick,
here I am. I have a life here.

Our ties remain strongest when they are sustained by
both proximity and mutual need. In *A Crown of Glory: A Biblical View of Aging,* Rachel Dulin cites sections of the Book of
Ruth depicting a model of aging in which "older members
of the family were a resource, not a liability." She suggests
that through older relatives' essential contributions to
child-rearing "a balance of function, usefulness, and purpose was attained both in the family unit and in the community."[6]

Ironically, divorce has become so widespread in modern societies that assistance from grandparents has become
necessary again. In their study of grandparents' relations
with their families, the researchers Andrew Cherlin and
Frank Furstenberg found that the high divorce rate is asso-
ciated with close relationships between grandparents and
grandchildren. They observe that "strong, functional intergenerational ties are linked to family crises, low incomes,
and instability."[7]

In modern industrial societies, we tend to acknowledge the truth of our dependence on one another only
when illness or another stressful event makes this reality
fully evident to us. Nancy Foner, an anthropologist, notes
in contrast that people in nonindustrial societies regularly
rely on each other "in times of emergency, disaster, or danger," and that they "must depend on, and cultivate and
maintain a large array of social relationships as a resource
throughout their lives."[8] She points out that there is little
discontinuity between the beginning, middle, and end of

life when only the nature of one's dependency changes, but not the certainty of it.

FRIENDSHIP AND EXHAUSTION

Much conspires against friendship in later life. Retirement removes the context from which work friendships may have drawn their momentum. Physical problems may interfere with the nature of our activities and the frequency of our contacts with others. Above all, the deaths of old friends may rob us of the will for friendship. A sixty-eight-year-old woman states flatly, "My close friends are either dead or live at a great distance and I have no interest in making new ones."[9]

We become weary when old friends die. After the deaths of several friends and relatives in succession, the poet Emily Dickinson wrote in a letter to a friend, "The Dyings have been too deep for me, and before I could raise my Heart from one, another has come."[10] She died a few months later at the age of fifty-six. The very notion of replacing an old friend feels false, since it is impossible to match in a short span something that became what it was because of the passage of decades. When new friends beckon, we are reluctant to put in the heart and the energy, only to have death again deny our harvest.

Many people limit themselves to superficial friendships at the end of their lives. They insist that nothing further is possible, staying within safe conversational topics, such as the doings of family members and the trivialities of medical problems. They then point to these dull friendships as proof of their initial belief. An eighty-one-year-old woman claims, "When you're older you don't go deep into friendship." She continues:

What do you hear from any of us? My family, my children, my grandchildren—that's all you hear. You have no place to grow together. When you're younger you do. You're educating your children, having a social life with your husband. . . . When you're older, you've heard it all before . . . and anyway, what more is there to say?[11]

Some of the worst rejections received in later life come from other older people. A man who was unhappy with his move to a retirement home wrote, "Most people here are either senile, hard of hearing, unable to speak above a whisper, [or] 'slow on the trigger.' "[12] All of us see aging more readily in strangers than in ourselves. Into our own faces and the faces of people we have known for years we infuse the memories of youth and early adulthood. For strangers, there can be no interposing of a past that was never witnessed. Especially when age has wreaked disfigurement, we see the disability before we see the person.

A seventy-year-old resident of a retirement home attests to the hurt caused by such attitudes:

I used to go down to the lobby for coffee hour, but it was too hard for me to hear what people were saying. If more than one talks at once, forget it—I can't hear a thing. They all laugh, and I don't know what's so funny. You feel like an idiot, nodding and smiling when you don't know what the heck is going on. I can't keep asking people to repeat things for me. As it is, I can tell I'm a burden to have around. I can picture them saying under their breaths when they see me, "Oh, no, look who's coming." So I don't go any more. It's not worth it.

We tend to shun in others what we fear in ourselves. Yet mustering our willingness to look beneath the surface of other people's infirmities is the only way to counter this fear with hope. If instead we keep averting our eyes and refusing to make accommodations, our intolerance will fill us with dread as our own surface deteriorates. We may leave ourselves stranded.

The first rule of change is dissatisfaction. The word sad is derived from the Old English *saed* for sated and the Latin *satis* for enough. Satiation, or running out of wants, is a living death. When we are satisfied that we know all that is worth knowing about ourselves, or when we accept that there is nothing more to say or to learn from others, we close off our curiosity. We tell ourselves, "I've had enough," and we stay sad and exhausted.

I once knew a group of women in a nursing home who reached a point of utter fatigue from talking about their children, grandchildren, pills, and bowel problems. One day, they vowed that when they came together for meals, they would each bring something to the conversation outside of the familial and bodily domain. One of the women described what happened:

> The first dinner was terrible. We had nothing to say. But we were all stubborn enough to keep our promise. We ate in complete silence. The next morning, a few of us brought newspaper clippings with us to breakfast, and one woman brought along a poem she'd written. It was like lighting a fire. We just needed to get started, and then it went. Each day got easier. Pretty soon, the whole dining room envied us. Everyone stared over at our table and wondered what was going on that was so interesting. So much came out of us, but we had to push ourselves to do it.

Taking an interest is half of inspiration. A woman whose vision and hearing had both markedly diminished decided to force herself to go to a senior center, reasoning "If I don't go soon, I wouldn't recognize a new friend if I could find one."[13] After moving to a retirement home an eighty-year-old woman wrote: "An unexpected pleasure was finding so many friends of like age and interests. There was no need to be bored if one were interested in living."[14]

Three years before she died, the writer Lou Andreas-Salome befriended a younger man who stood by her loyally until her death. She wrote, "I find it nice of life that it always, even so late as this, sends something so exquisite for companionship along the way." Her biographer adds:

> The importance she had for this younger friend seems to have been due to that same power so many had noted in her before and which she evidently kept to the very end of her life—her power as an "understand-er" and listener. [He] visited her day after day and was quietly encouraged by her to talk about feelings, impressions, experiences. Often during these conversations he would think she had fallen asleep and he would stop talking, but then would hear her wholly attentive voice in the half-dark asking him to go on.[15]

As life gets physically more difficult, we need commitments to others to bind us to life. Those who stay insular find that their spirit for life dwindles along with their physical powers. In *The Gift*, Lewis Hyde maintains that gifts have to move from one person to another, or they lose their value: "Anything contained within a boundary must contain as well its own exhaustion. . . . The gift that is not used will be lost, while the one that is passed along remains abundant."[16] The gift of continuing to be alive, when passed on to others through friendship, makes the spirit abundant even as the body wanes.

Many people surprise themselves with the quality of

the friendships they are able to form, once they put aside their biases. A sixty-year-old man living in specialized housing for older and disabled people told me about the changes that were set in motion once he became receptive to making friendships there:

> I never thought I'd end up in a place like this. I've always been a loner. I never needed anybody's help and that's the way I wanted to keep it. But my stroke wiped me out. My savings were blown on all those doctor bills, and I couldn't get anyone to give me a job. So I moved in here. Boy, was I a snob. For the first couple of years, I didn't associate with any of these people. See, I was too young to be an old man, and I wasn't the kind to be on the dole. I had to prove I wasn't one of them. But it gradually dawned on me that we were all in the same boat. Everyone's here for a reason. Once I dropped my attitude, people came out of the woodwork to be friendly to me. I have more friends now than in my whole life put together.

Having witnessed similar transformations, Arlie Hochschild in *The Unexpected Community* portrays her observations of the relationships between residents in a senior apartment complex. She describes a sibling-like equality and reciprocity, claiming that during "some periods of life, such as adolescence and old age . . . an individual is open to, and needs, these back up relationships."[17]

A GENIUS FOR LIFE

A son wrote this account of his mother's triumphant use of dissatisfaction:

> My mother was fifty-five years old when she retired. She decided to take up swimming for exercise and

something to do, but she couldn't understand why the women who went swimming never interacted with each other in the dressing room or the pool. She made a decision: to go there and start talking. She found that many of the women were lonely, depressed, and isolated because of widowhood, fatigue from caregiving to sick husbands, or from their own aches and pains. Many of the women had led interesting lives: there was a singer with an operatic voice, a survivor of the Holocaust, an actress, and several former teachers. What began as a decision by one person became a small group of friends who swam together regularly and eventually became a group of eighty. They called themselves "The Aquabelles," and held a yearly dinner at a local restaurant in which many of the women performed. One subgroup did shows for nursing homes and another gave swimming lessons to children. Before my mother died, I asked her how she wanted to be remembered. She said she would like a simple plaque with a mermaid on it and the inscription, "Irma Delehanty, Aquabelle."

The words genius and generous come from the Latin root *genere*, meaning "to beget."[18] To have a genius for life is to possess the ability to generate warmth and well-being in others. This woman's generosity spawned similar impulses in her fellow swimmers, inspiring them to take an interest in each other and in projects greater than their individual concerns. Largess literally enlarges our lives.

Recovering or first discovering one's genius for life requires a convergence of opportunity and willingness. During the year following his mother's death, a son worried constantly about his eighty-six-year-old father. As often as he could, he made the two-hundred mile trip to the rural area where his father lived. He tells what he observed:

Within a month, he had hired a woman to clean his house and do the shopping. She's a single mother of two young children, so he had her bringing them along with her to the house to save on day care. My father is a practical man. He would watch the kids while she did the housework, and he got attached to them. A few months later, he was telling me how they lived in a cabin with no electricity, and how the kids got scared before the lamps were lit. The next thing I heard, he was having electricity installed for them. He said, "What else do I have to do with my money?" That's all he talks about now when I call—how his little family is doing. And when he was sick for a week and I couldn't get up there, this woman and her kids came every day to look after him. I don't think he could have gotten through his grief without them to fuss and fume about, and I think they would do anything for him.

The immediate genius of generosity is that it draws us out of ourselves. Leaving the confines of his loss, this man was carried away by his interest in the welfare of "his little family." Ecstasy, to be beside oneself with joy, is to have left the blunting boundaries of self-interest.

Generosity pulls us out of despondency, whether we arrive at this bonus accidentally or seek it intentionally. In circumstances when there is little we can do to improve our own lives, having a beneficial effect on someone else's life is especially encouraging to the spirit. In *Helplessness,* Martin Seligman writes, "I suggest that joy accompanies and motivates effective responding; . . . that what produces self-esteem and a sense of competence, and protects against depression, is not only the absolute quality of experience, but the perception that one's own actions controlled the experience."[19]

A sixty-one-year-old woman enduring dialysis three times a week explains:

On the other days, I'm a volunteer companion to housebound people. I keep them company, get them groceries, whatever. Look, I have the strength, and they can't get out. And it's a lifesaver for me. We laugh, we talk, we have lunch, sometimes we just watch TV. Otherwise, I'd have nothing to think about but my next dialysis.

During her long hours on the kidney machine, this woman thinks about the people who count on her. She imagines special treats she will pick up for them at the store or comes up with ideas that will help them to flourish. Her capacity to endure arises directly from her stake in other people's survival. Knowing that her actions make a difference protects her from depression and assures her that her life continues to serve a purpose.

Accepting help from others and allowing them to feel that their contributions are significant is its own generosity. In doing so, we affirm the ongoing value of good will and the fact that thoughtfulness is never wasted. A woman who coped with polio for most of her life explains:

When my neighbors ring my bell on a snowy day to inquire if I need something from the store, even though I am prepared for bad weather I try to think up some item rather than reject a generous offer. It is kinder to accept help than refuse it in an effort to prove independence.[20]

It is in the nature of kindness that both the helper and the helped exchange encouragement. In *The First Year Alone,* Beverly Gordon describes how she was unable to extricate herself from depression after her husband died. Mercifully, a friend urged her to hire as her housekeeper a young woman who needed to be taught basic living skills, such as cooking, budgeting, and shopping. After a few months, the young woman's daily need for her brought her predicament to the fore: she had to choose between dwelling on her loss and opening herself to the risks and rewards of a fresh attachment. She concluded, "No matter how deep my sorrow may be, it does not give me license to waste the rest of my life."[21]

Engaging life requires an active decision; letting ourselves languish requires little effort. After uprooting herself in order to move into low-cost housing, an eighty-year-old woman describes the lassitude that resulted:

> I wake up in the morning and start to get up. Then I ask myself: What for? Because I have nothing to do any more—no dog, no garden, nobody to take care of. And I don't eat. I cook something for the evening and when it is ready, I say ach! I don't want to eat it, and I put it in the refrigerator.[22]

The writer Robertson Davies claims that lethargy is one of the greatest dangers we face as we age. Having become disenchanted with many aspects of life, we may pull back into a state of protective indifference in which we decrease our exposure to pain, but also bypass chances to be invigorated. He writes, "There is only one kind of failure that really breaks the spirit. . . . It is the failure which manifests itself in a loss of interest in really important things. . . . Once it has us in its grip, it is hard for us to recognize what ails us."[23]

I once asked a wheelchair-bound resident of a nursing home the secret of her consistent good spirits. She answered:

> Friends. I've made a few good ones here. My brain, my mouth, and my heart still work, so I use them. Take the aide who dresses me in the morning—she's having a hard time of it in her life. I always get to hear the latest about her sons and her ex-husband. Sometimes I put

my two cents in. Mostly, I just listen so she can get it off her chest. I've got all the time in the world, so she pours her heart out. She does extra things for me, like get me nightgowns with ties in the back instead of snaps. She likes to see that I'm comfortable, and I like to nudge her into making a better life for herself.

In drawing out the aide's story, this woman turned a degrading chore into a daily interlude of camaraderie. She made something out of the nothingness of life in a nursing home.

No matter how severely our other powers decline, the capacity to attract and sustain friendship is a constructive force that need not leave us. In *The Art Spirit,* Robert Henri claims that genius "exists in some degree in everyone" and that "any material will do."[24] The genius in generosity does not depend on perishable resources like wealth, beauty, or physical mobility. We can extend ourselves to whoever is at hand.

§

Prior to getting sick, many people insist that becoming more and more independent is a sign of progress in life. They regard the need to lean on others as a weakness or as an indication of decline. In *The Evolving Self,* Robert Kegan counters such views by suggesting that we all experience a lifelong yearning for "integration, attachment, inclusion."[25] He maintains that this need develops in tandem with our urge for autonomy, no matter how ardently we try to suppress or ignore it.

An eighty-one-year-old woman who endured three heart attacks in six years explains how she sustains herself:

I never sit still if I know somebody who needs me. I have a lady on the seventh floor. I do different things for her, like washing her hair and making lunch for her. She loves peanut butter. Every night I walk her up and down the corridor so she gets her exercise. If she don't exercise, she'll get sick and be sent to a nursing home. I also do her laundry when she's not feeling up to it, which is most of the time. This lady is only seventy-two years old. She could be my little sister. But she has no family, no one to look in on her. The people in this building, we're her family.[26]

NINE

Prospects for Revival

Alan Jabbour, a historian of music, spent several years documenting the lives of folk artists around the country. He found that "many of America's finest folk artists are old people," observing:

> I was a little surprised to hear from the old fiddlers I first encountered that several of them had stopped playing for twenty or thirty years, then begun again recently. Each had his reasons, of course. One quit because his wife could not stand the music. For another, the combined burdens of long work hours and raising a big family simply crowded the fiddle out. . . . By the time I had heard thirty versions of the story from fiddlers scattered across the Upper South, I began to realize that something bigger and more fundamental was going on. . . . I was learning that old age was precisely when one played the fiddle.[1]

There are rich prospects for revival in the privileges granted by a slowed-down body and a less-crowded mind. Resuming activities that we gave up during the commotion of our earlier years may renew our spirit for life. Discovering previously untapped abilities and pursuing their development may inspire us with fresh purposes. A ninety-year-old weaver from New Mexico states, "I love to weave. I'll stop weaving when I can't move any more. Until then, you'll find me dancing on the loom."[2]

This chapter explores the possibilities that arise once physical problems have reduced our choices and stripped away previously dominant aspects of our identity. In an essay, "Psychotherapy and the Patient with a Limited Life-Span," Lawrence LeShan and Eda LeShan assert: "If a person has one hour to live and discovers himself and his life in that hour, is not this a valid and important growth? . . . There are no deadlines on living, none on what one may do or feel so long as one is alive."[3] Illness or old age may disrupt so many of the patterns that previously constrained us that we may at last attain the freedom to be fully ourselves.

DISCERNING PURPOSES

We do not take well to uselessness. An eighty-year-old psychiatrist writes about his retirement and his subsequent visits back to the hospital unit that he pioneered:

> I have become painfully aware that absence does *not* make the heart grow fonder. There is an entirely understandable and healthy tendency for the staff to regroup after the loss of a leading figure and to find a new identity they can call their own. When I visit . . . I really am an interloper in *their* hospital. Moreover, they want to describe *their* achievements largely without reference to the past. I respect this truth as an important aspect of their collective self-image, but it still leaves a vacuum for me—and just a little pain at the reminder that I'm a has-been.[4]

Retirement and illness challenge us to redefine what it means to be of use and to have a purpose. Outside of making a living, raising a family, or practicing the trade or profession around which we have built our identity, most of us would be hard-pressed to designate other aims. A woman describing herself as "an old social worker" protests, "How retire? One does not incorporate a professional self for some forty years only to cast it off suddenly as a worn outer garmet. It was my flesh and blood, giving meaning and purpose to my life."[5]

Our lives are structured such that grappling with emptiness is usually concentrated at the end. In youth, our time is filled with schooling. Middle age is consumed with work, and the last third of life is left to leisure. Younger people crave work and free time, middle-aged people long for leisure and opportunities to learn, and older people wish above all for useful activity and new knowledge. A woman in her eighties writes, "I could wipe out ninety percent of old people's woes at a stroke by finding them suitable work. . . . Real work and real education, that's the open secret of satisfaction from birth to death."[6]

What counts as "real work" is an individual question. Activities such as teaching, creating things of beauty, or helping other people are highly esteemed by some while held in low regard by others. Those accustomed to more concrete purposes may not be satisfied with the kinds of work they are able to do within their reduced physical capacities. A sixty-nine-year-old man asserts that what is needed during retirement is "a willingness to accept a kind of excommunication from the things from which one formerly derived satisfaction."[7]

A stumbling-block for many is that the work available to them is unpaid. A retired man writes, "I've always believed that the laborer is worthy of his hire, that you get what you pay for. . . . So it is very hard for me to believe that people really value my work when I do it for nothing.'"[8]. Assigning worth to a task according to the amount of money received is an attitude not easily discarded, no matter how vehemently reassurances are offered that one's unpaid work is valued.

The psychologist George Kelly suggests that we each employ personal constructs, customary channels through which our thoughts reach conclusions, and that these constructs limit what we are able to perceive. He writes, "When [a person] is under pressure he is not likely to develop new channels; instead he will tend to reverse himself along the dimensional lines which have already been established."[9] A man who had been a successful packaging designer had a stroke in which he lost the use of his right hand. He recounts a painful moment of reckoning that occurred soon after his return home from the hospital:

> I was home alone. I can't recall the exact circumstances but I suspect I must have tried to do something with my right arm and failed. Then it hit me—the realization I'd been trying to deny since I'd had my stroke. I was going to be crippled for the rest of my life. They say that your past life flashes before you when you're drowning. I don't know about that, but it certainly happened to me with this realization.[10]

Seeing his situation in such dire terms left this man choiceless and bereft. Contained in the designs he had rendered with his right hand had been all he knew of his talents and all he had surmised about making a meaningful life. Eventually, he realized that there was more to him and to life than had emerged in his previous career, but much time and struggle elapsed before he was able to widen his views to this extent.

Once the initial pressures of illness or idleness abate, our old ways of perceiving may gradually fall away. A woman who was diagnosed with multiple sclerosis at the age of thirty-seven states, "The knowledge that I have MS has acted primarily as a great clarifier. It has . . . accelerated the process of stripping down that I think usually occurs as we age. Having MS has made me want to be even more clear about exactly what life is and to be direct in my response to it."[11]

Some people find that they are satisfied by the sheer pleasure of being in the midst of activity. A seventy-five-year-old man with emphysema found that his need was to be around people, to absorb the color and commotion of lives being actively lived:

> I used to be an engineer. Now I drive an airport van for a hotel. Sometimes I have a lot of work and other times I'm hardly busy at all. That's the way I like it. I'm not obligated every day, every hour, but it gets me out into the world, with people. After my wife died, I had to find something to do. If I'd stayed home, it would've killed me. I look forward to going to work. You wouldn't believe all the crazy stories people tell me while I drive them around. It's hard for me to lift their bags, with all my huffing and puffing, but it's worth it. I feel like I'm still part of the human race.

To feel that their lives are worthwhile, others need to participate in something larger than themselves. They need to know that somewhere, at least for a few hours a week, their presence is expected and their efforts make a difference. A woman who serves as a foster grandparent claims that being in the program has made her feel "alive again. I get up in the morning and say, 'I gotta go see my children.'" Another woman in the program explains, "Being a volunteer has given me a new lease on life. There's no reason why one should sit back and vegetate because one has reached a certain age. . . . There's meaning in what I do."[12]

Until we manage to redefine our purposes in this way, our days may lose their momentum and our spirits may yield to lassitude. A fifty-three-year-old man was forced to retire from his position as a corporate executive due to worsening multiple sclerosis. For the next several months, he dreamt all night long that he was at work, and he felt envious and degraded each morning as he watched his wife leave for her job. After struggling through the chasm of having nothing to do, he eventually emerged with another view of his circumstances:

> It started with an elderly neighbor asking me for help doing her taxes. I'd gotten to feeling so worthless that I was surprised she thought of me. Then another neighbor needed help doing her budget. She'd gotten into bad debt with credit cards, so started coming over once a month to figure out how to match her income with her expenses. Then a friend asked my advice in managing his stocks. It kept building like that. Now I have about ten or fifteen regular clients. They come here, right to my living room, because I can't get to them. I do everything from balancing checkbooks to managing stock portfolios. Some of them want to pay me, but I don't want their money. They're already giving me much more than I give them.

This man was finally able to relinquish his previous notions of a useful life and replace them with ideas that fit his circumstances. Many of the crises of the latter half of life are marked by desperate bids to retain old channels of satisfaction and fulfillment. It is only when we let go of the familiar that fresh life can come in and revive us.

AGELESSNESS

Our chronological age misleads us. We can be deceived by numerical certainty into believing that the sum of our lived years tells us something absolute and incontestable about ourselves. A ninety-year-old woman insists, "Some folks are born old and some never get old."[13] A seventy-three-year-old man writes, "For the past thirty years I have felt rather ageless. I did, however, feel 'old' and troubled in my youth."[14] A woman in her eighties explains:

> You know, to be eighty is nothing to dread, because at eighty you can be the age of whoever you talk to. If I'm with my grandchildren, the little ones, I understand them because I've been there and I know. If I'm with a twenty-four-year-old mother with young babies, I know exactly what she's talking about. I feel like I'm her age and I can understand her world. That's one of the nice things about being old. You're the age of whoever you're with.[15]

As a result of illness or retirement, the open time and emotional spaciousness of childhood are often returned to us, but not childhood's unquestioning ease of play, laughter, and imagination. A seventy-four-year-old former university professor recalls that his "greatest problem" when he first retired was "shifting from a heavy-pressured, overly structured life to one of free form choices."[16] A man who was forced by Parkinson's disease to retire at the age of forty-eight writes: "When I was employed, the routines required by work shaped . . . what time I got up, when I ate my meals, when I went to the bathroom, when I could relax. . . . But upon retirement, I nearly drowned in an ocean of decisions to be made."[17]

Recovering childhood's ease with open time requires

that we first renew our other child-like capacities. These may have languished in us over the years, to the point of having been forgotten or suppressed beyond immediate retrieval. In *Growing Young*, Ashley Montagu celebrates the qualities of open-mindedness, resilience, a sense of wonder, and enthusiasm as "the most valuable possessions of our species, to be cherished, nurtured, and cultivated."[18]

People who evince agelessness in their manner of living are those who have retained child-like qualities throughout adulthood or have managed to accomplish their recovery. Asked what she regarded as the reason for her longevity, a hundred-year-old woman explained, "I think my sense of humor has protected me from stress. My favorite motto on aging is this: 'Age is a question of mind over matter. If you don't mind, it won't matter.' "[19]

As one of our earliest and most enduring capacities, laughter can help lead us back into childhood's ease. At least momentarily, we loosen our hold on ourselves. In *Anatomy of an Illness*, Norman Cousins recounts what happened when he began watching humorous movies in his hospital room: "Nothing is less funny than being flat on your back with all the bones in your spine and joints hurting. . . . [But] it worked. I made the joyous discovery that ten minutes of genuine belly laughter had an anesthetic effect."[20]

A physician who studied the beneficial effects of humor on illness states, "Perhaps ultimately, and in the deepest sense, humor works by rallying, and by being a manifestation of, the will to live." He cites the case of a ninety-five-year-old man who was admitted to the hospital with severe depression:

He had not eaten for several days and for the same period had not said a word to anyone. His physicians were alarmed; they were concerned that he would soon die. A clown entered his hospital room and within thirty minutes had succeeded in getting the elderly man to talk, to laugh, and to eat. The man lived for several more years and the clown maintained communication with him during this time.[21]

Laughter brings us back to the present moment, to the sheer fact of continuing to be alive and viewing the spectacle around us. In a similar way, pets invigorate us by demanding our attention and obliging us to act on their behalf. The philosopher Arthur Schopenhauer asserts, "[Pets] are the present moment personified, and in some respects they make us feel the value of every hour that is free from trouble and annoyance."[22] A seventy-nine-year-old woman living with severe heart disease explains:

> To tell you the truth, the reason I get up in the morning is my dog. When I feel him licking my face, I smile—even when I have no use for anything else in the world. He needs to be walked, fed, petted, loved, so I get out of bed. For him, I take my pills, otherwise my legs would swell so much I wouldn't be able to make it around the block. He needs the exercise, so I get the exercise.

At the end of Ingmar Bergman's film, "Fanny and Alexander," the eldest character makes an impassioned plea to the younger members of his family: "We must live in the little, the little world. We shall be content with that and cultivate it and make the best of it. . . . It is necessary, and not in the least shameful, to take pleasure in . . . good food, gentle smiles, fruit-trees in bloom, waltzes."[23]

Such simplicity becomes complicated in adulthood. It is often difficult to recognize when we have had enough of the larger world and can cease trying to reach beyond that which is within our immediate grasp. The Chinese philosopher Lao Tzu writes, "No calamity is greater / Than not knowing what is enough. / No fault worse than wanting too much. / Whoever knows what is enough / Has enough."[24]

The intrusion of death in our affairs may prove to us that it is enough to go on living and to take pleasure where we can find it. After his father's funeral, a forty-two-year-old man returned to the house where both he and his father had been raised and in which his grandfather and father had died. He spent a long time in his father's study, sitting at his desk and looking at the photographs of the successive childhoods that had been contained in that house. Later, he recorded the insights that came to him during those hours:

> Childhood, the origin of life, is the originality a person brings to every stage in life. . . . The ordeals of ageing are certainly among the adult necessities with which a person has got to cope, but the lively survival of the child in the adult is a potent resource for coping with them. . . . Childhood is life's laughter, its hurt, its rage, its capacity for play, its boundless imagination, its lyrical sense of the future.[25]

Even if buried under the travails of many decades, resources like laughter and wonder can be summoned back at any point in life. At age sixty-two, the Canadian painter Emily Carr noted in her journal, "I feel old, old, old and stiff and tired, except when I paint; then I'm no age."[26] Our joyful capacities are not bound to a particular stage of life any more than are our faculties for sorrow, love, or anger. Reclaiming them is our best hope for animating ourselves in circumstances otherwise demeaning or depleting.

A FULL AND FINAL EMERGENCE

Much of life consists of shedding all that interferes with the expression of our uniqueness. Our individual voice is always distinctive; the difficulty lies in finding what we are, free of artifice. A fifty-two-year-old daughter describes her mother's unexpected growth late in life:

> My mother's always been a loner. When she was almost seventy, someone roped her into going to a discussion group at a senior center. I couldn't believe that she went in the first place. Then she started going every week. Over the phone, she'd tell me what this one said and that one said, like it was a soap opera or something. I never thought she had it in her, but she really got caught up in other people's lives. And she's been telling me a thing or two about herself, just throwing it into the conversation every so often. Listening to other people, hearing what they have to say about their lives, really loosened her up. After all these years, I'm actually getting to know my own mother. I guess it's never too late to change.

We may find at the end of life that our curiosity and our craving for self-expression speak louder than our reticence. As a function of our full and final emergence, much of what once restrained us may recede in importance. We may no longer feel bound by the need to compete, conform, or seek approval, allowing us to express ourselves more completely than ever before. The pianist Artur Rubinstein remarked, "I am eighty. So now I take chances I never took before. You see, the stakes are not so high. I can afford it. I used to be so much more careful. No wrong notes. Not too bold ideas. . . . Now I let go and enjoy myself and to hell with everything but the music!"[27]

Rudolf Arnheim, an author and art historian, notes that artists who are able to embrace their aging develop a "late style" which takes advantage of the "withdrawal and inflexibility" of old age. In an interview recorded when Arnheim was eighty-four years old, he suggests that inflexibility is often an evolved version of confidence.[28] Through years of searching and experimenting, such artists arrive at an inner certainty toward their work which leaves them free both of others' opinions and their own doubts.

Finding a distinctive style late in life is no less significant for its being delayed. Pressures to measure ourselves against others never completely cease, but many of us strengthen our liberation the closer we get to the end of our lives. A woman in her eighties writes, "Perhaps the most exciting facet of aging . . . is that heady sense of emancipation, of having arrived at full identity."[29] Another woman writes:

> I leave room now, at sixty-five, for the unexpected. That was not always true of me. I used to feel I was in a kind of linear race with life and time. . . . There were landmarks placed by other generations, and I had to arrive on time or fail in the whole race. If I didn't pass—if the sixth grade went on to the seventh without me, I would be one year behind for the rest of my life. If I graduated from high school in 1928, I had to graduate from college in 1932. When I didn't graduate from college until 1951, it took me another twenty years to realize the preceding twenty years weren't lost.[30]

Many people possess talents that they hold in reserve until their obligations to others have been fulfilled or until life quiets down enough to allow them finally to heed their own inclinations. A gerontologist observes, "The ending of a job or career, the maturation of children, and newly gained time may permit the expression of a 'true' personality and interests, allowing one to act in new and inventive ways."[31]

A woman in her early sixties experienced "a tremendous release" as part of her bereavement after her husband's death. During their forty-two-year marriage, she notes, "I almost destroyed myself as a person. . . . Everything I did centered around my home, husband, and sons." During her first year of widowhood, she attended a poetry workshop where her pent-up feelings emerged:

> I could write and it was not too bad! It was as if I were born again into another body and for the first time in my life I felt good about being me, a unique, interesting person with some talent of my own. . . . I am still learning, growing, and evolving into my real self. I find I am happiest when I am in any kind of a learning experience, be it a classroom, lecture, or just reading and writing. Time passes swiftly and I started late. It is so great to continue to grow. I do not expect to be a great writer and do not write for a living but write in order to live.[32]

For women who have devoted most of their adulthood to aiding their husbands' careers and raising children, the last third of life can be as frightening as it is expansive. In *Women of a Certain Age*, Lillian Rubin speaks for the generations of women who came of age prior to the women's movement: "Like so many others, I awoke one day from the childhood dream that I would be forever cared for—that being some man's wife and some child's mother would occupy my mind and my hands for the rest of my life."[33] Starting out with empty hands, many women find themselves bursting in their last years with previously unknown capacities.

Men from these generations often experience a paral-

lel liberation. Released from earning a living and comply-
ing with others' expectations, many celebrate the absence
of responsibilities and interpersonal constraints. One
homebound eighty-year-old man states, "Sitting here is just
something to do. . . . But I like it: there's nothing I'd rather
be doing. With sitting—and with everything else—I'm free
to follow my moods. There's no one else here to tell me
what to do."[34]

When life slows down, we become especially free to en-
gage in worlds of our own making. In "The Life Review: An
Interpretation of Reminiscence in the Aged," Robert Butler writes, "Probably at no other time of life is there as potent a force toward self-awareness operating as in old age."[35]
A woman who decided to become a painter at the age of
eighty-three writes: "Detailed scenes were projecting themselves in my mind, windows of the past, waiting to be
opened. . . . Ideas seemed to tumble over themselves in my
mind, anxious to be put on canvas. Soon the walls of my
apartment were covered with bright paintings."[36]

At any age, recovering and discovering ourselves require the same willingness to heed our quiet yearnings. Illness and old age are exceptional in the quietude that they
supply, yet we can choose to create similar conditions earlier in our lives. In *Solitude: A Return to the Self,* the psychiatrist Anthony Storr describes an approach he takes with
middle-aged patients suffering from depression:

> Such patients are often people who, because of the de-
> mands of their careers and families, have neglected or
> abandoned pursuits and interests which, at an earlier
> point in time, gave life zest and meaning. If the patient
> is encouraged to recall what made life meaningful to
> him in adolescence, he will begin to discover neglected
> sides of himself, and perhaps turn once again to music,

or to painting, or to some other cultural or intellectual pursuit which once enthralled him, but which the pressure of life's business had made him abandon.[37]

Taking back our earlier yearnings, or daring to develop them for the first time, is one of the key privileges of having time on our hands. Playing music for the pleasure of it, learning to dance for the sensation of it, or painting for the adventure of it are the kind of activities that we may abandon to our detriment during our busy middle years. A seventy-five-year-old woman notes, "When you think that it takes nine months to grow a baby, it's not surprising that it takes seventy years and more to grow a soul."[38]

Jim Heynen, a writer, and Paul Boyer, a photographer, interviewed a hundred people who were over a hundred years old. They describe one man whose "best days" over the course of a long lifetime seemed to be his last:

> He's had poor eyesight his whole life, worked menial jobs most of his working years, and spent most of his long marriage in the shadow of a wife who did most of the talking, which was okay with him. Only recently, in the space and silence of extreme old age, has he come into his own—telling stories. He's a great storyteller, and seems to be surprising himself as much as the people around him with a talent that has finally begun to bloom.[39]

§

Between the ages of eighty-three and ninety-six, a man who dedicated himself to painting "one masterpiece a day" jotted these comments in letters to friends:

> Painting and sketching keep me busy and interested— always with a desire to improve. . . . It's fun to be alive and to be contributing something, however little, *but*

still something. . . . After finishing a canvas—I always hope—the next one will be better. Still so much to learn. . . . I am not an amateur nor a professional—nor a hobbyist or a Sunday painter—I'm a free lance and paint because I love it so.[40]

CONCLUSION

The Measure of a Good Life

After undergoing surgery for prostate cancer, the critic Anatole Broyard wrote:

> What a critically ill person needs above all is to be understood. Dying is a misunderstanding you have to get straightened out before you go. And you can't be understood, your situation can't be appreciated, until your family and friends, staring at you with an embarrassed love, come to know, with an intimate, absolute knowledge, what your illness is like.[1]

In this book, I have used stories more than studies in an effort to capture some of the ineffable aspects of illness and disability. I have not represented every view, but I have tried to assemble a variety of insights in a way that rings true to the experience of dependency and to the inner transformations it produces. Only ill and disabled people can judge how closely I have verged on their experience.

When I began writing, I did not know where the exploration of these themes would take me. I followed the lead of my patients and the personal testimonies in the literature of illness and disability. Through three years of writing, thinking, and reading, I found my way to aspects of illness that needed to be described. Mark Twain once jotted in his notebook: "The time to begin writing an article is when you have finished it to your satisfaction. By that time you begin to clearly and logically perceive what it is that you really want to say."[2]

Every attempt to explain how we cope with hardship contains its own definition of successful aging and there-fore its own idea of what constitutes a good life. These defi-nitions are not always stated outright, yet they determine what researchers choose to measure in their studies and what therapists choose to explore in their sessions. In *Old, Sick, and Helpless: Where Therapy Begins,* Robert Kastenbaum and his co-authors suggest that a therapist's personal belief system is most urgently challenged by working with those who do not have long to live. They write:

> For the therapist working with the frail and infirm aged, the philosophical questions are never absent. One can hardly get through the day without drawing upon a philosophy of care that, in turn, flows from a general philosophy of life. It is not an indulgence for the geriatric therapist to be philosophical; it is a neces-sity.[3]

In this last chapter, I offer my view of aging and living well. My philosophy of life has necessarily permeated the structure and content of the book as a whole, influencing my selection of stories and my choice of texts used to sup-port my argument. An author cannot escape personal bias, but at least can make its contours clear.

AGING WELL

Helplessness has become the dreaded underside of modern life, out of view and all the more harrowing for its unfamiliarity. It is now possible to go through the first half and sometimes the first two-thirds of life having no direct contact with someone who is seriously ill. In contrast, traditional cultures mark the occurrence of illness and death through public rituals which keep these aspects of life conspicuous. In *The Hour of Our Death,* an account of how dying has been handled over the centuries, Philippe Aries entitles the last section about modern times, "The Invisible Death." He writes, "Except for the death of statesmen, society has banished death. In the towns, there is no way of knowing that something has happened. . . . Society no longer observes a pause; the disappearance of an individual no longer affects its continuity."[4]

A man in his forties whose older brother had recently died told his therapist:

> I feel as though my whole life was built on a frozen lake. We all go on with our activities. We work on the house and play golf and entertain and have our fights. I put in long hours at work and think I'm doing well. Then every once in a while I think, "This is ice I'm standing on and it's melting."[5]

Many people try to flee such feelings, rather than attempting to come to terms with them. In *The Atman Project,* Ken Wilber writes: "No amount of compensations . . . is enough to finally and totally screen out this background dread. . . . An individual will create, or latch on to, a whole host of external or objective wants, desires, properties, and possessions, goods and materials."[6] Attempting to flee dread only intensifies it. From then on, we have to keep averting our eyes from further evidence of physical deterioration and suffering. The work of avoidance itself becomes consuming.

When a friend or relative becomes ill, we have the choice of participating in the care or backing away. Taking the time to give assistance may run counter to the pace or the ostensible purpose of our lives. The organizing principle of modern life has become almost wholly economic. In *The Human Condition,* Hannah Arendt writes: "We have almost succeeded in leveling all human activities to the common denominator of securing the necessities of life and providing for their abundance. Whatever we do, we are supposed to do for the sake of 'making a living'; such is the verdict of society."[7]

Researchers who interviewed middle-class Americans from 1979 to 1984 found a pervasive devotion to individual purposes and a wariness toward getting involved in the lives of others. Expressing alarm toward what they saw as their informants' intense and exclusive fidelity to their private worlds, they suggest that individualism "has marched inexorably through our history" and that this ethos "may have grown cancerous."[8]

Only by actively opposing this ethos can we make frailty less frightening. Earlier in our lives, we must stop clinging to independence as if it were the only meaning of strength. In this respect, women may fare better than men. David McClelland, a psychologist, reviewed the literature on gender differences, finding that "women are quicker to recognize their own interdependence; they are more interested in situations where interdependence is important."[9] In *In a Different Voice,* Carol Gilligan offers her findings from extensive interviews with men and women about their view of themselves. She reports that men tend to emphasize "separation as it defines and empowers the self" and women speak of "the ongoing process of attachment that creates and sustains the human community."[10]

We either face the truth of our fragility head-on, or we immerse ourselves still more intently in other priorities. There is no middle course, because spending time beside an ill person puts us into contact with the dire underside of life. In *The Denial of Death,* Ernest Becker portrays what we realize while sitting in the midst of the odors and sights of illness:

> Man is a worm and food for worms. This is the paradox: he is out of nature and hopelessly in it; he is dual, up in the stars and yet housed in a heart-pumping, breath-gasping body that once belonged to a fish and still carries the gill-marks to prove it. His body is a material fleshy casing that is alien to him in many ways— the strangest and most repugnant way being that it aches and bleeds and will decay and die. Man is literally split in two: he has an awareness of his own splendid uniqueness in that he sticks out of nature with a towering majesty, and yet goes back into the ground a few feet in order blindly and dumbly to rot and disappear forever. It is a terrifying dilemma to be in and have to live with.[11]

There is terror and relief in allowing this awareness to rear its full impact. We may begin to live in terms of, rather than in flight from, the approach of our ending. In *The Experience of Nothingness,* Michael Novak writes, "The drive to question allows the human animal to lift his eyes from the sequence of daily routines to perceive the law of his own death, and to struggle for ways of life that assuage death's bitterness."[12] After such experiences, changes may emerge in the way we spend our time, conduct our relationships, and look at the future.

A researcher interviewed forty-two women who had been the person in their family centrally responsible for the care of their ailing parents. Struck by the women's "relative ease and competence in handling their own old-age disabilities," the researcher concluded:

> The experience of nursing someone who is sick, dying, or disabled strips away, for most people, the mystery, horror, and disgust. . . . It is not surprising, therefore, that these [women], . . . who are deeply experienced in caring for sick parents in the latter's old age, tend to take their own sickness and disability in stride. They have known before in an intimate manner the difficulties they might encounter later in their own lives.[13]

Prior to getting sick or reaching advanced age, we can choose to grant ourselves a close acquaintance with physical suffering and its alleviation. We can draw near to the sickbeds of friends and relatives and involve ourselves in the experience of helplessness, hoping that this foreknowledge will help us to age well.

KINDNESS

In many respects, kindness does not make sense. In his essay, "Altruism," Lewis Thomas observes that this impulse "has always been one of biology's deep mysteries." He continues:

> At first glance, it seems an unnatural act, a violation of nature, to give away one's life, or even one's posses-

sions, to another. And yet, in the face of improbability, examples of altruism abound. . . . I maintain, despite the moment's evidence against the claim, that we are born and grow up with a fondness for each other, and we have genes for that. We can be talked out of it, for the genetic message is like a distant music and some of us are hard-of-hearing. Societies are noisy affairs, drowning out the sound of ourselves and our connection. . . . Nonetheless, the music is there, waiting for more listeners.[14]

Many people have difficulty believing in kindness as a human possibility. Past experience has taught them that other people are not to be trusted and that to accept help from someone is to open the door to exploitation. They avoid putting themselves in the vulnerable position of receiving throughout adulthood, building their identity around a core of aloneness. A physician specializing in the emotional aspects of living with cancer observes: "There are people who take pride in being self-reliant; independent men and women whose confidence and self-esteem derive largely from being able to say to themselves: 'I ask for no special favors; if need be, I can make it on my own.' Such individuals are especially threatened . . . [when] the sudden need to depend on another undermines the very foundations of their personal identity."[15]

Before we can fully believe in kindness, we have to experience it personally. In *Cruelty and Kindness,* Harvey Hornstein notes that "a person's conception of humanity's moral and ethical disposition is influenced by his or her specific encounters with other individuals."[16] The power of specific encounters is both the grounding of morality and the basis for hope in later life.

In our clinic, I have seen solitary, irascible people become soft and receptive in response to particularly tender members of our staff. Later, these individuals have said that our taking an interest in them gave them the impetus to make a better life for themselves. Some gave up self-destructive habits in direct response to the caring they received. In *Aging is a Lifelong Affair,* Ben Weininger observes:

> You need an experience with at least one person who cares about you. It doesn't matter at what age this person appears. If you didn't have a close relationship when younger, and you now have one close person in your life, that makes up for the early deficiency. That person can appear at any time in the life cycle, even on the day of death. One does not need to make up for lost time.[17]

A philosopher interested in the idea of goodness spent a decade trying to understand why certain residents of a tiny village in France opened their doors to Jewish refugees during the Holocaust. He wanted to find out what motivated this lifesaving minority. Their actions put them in danger of reprisal from the Nazis, yet they persisted in giving shelter throughout the war. This scholar's relentless questioning of these villagers yielded only the simplest explanations. He writes:

> When I asked [one of the villagers] why she found it necessary to let those refugees into her house, dragging after them all those dangers and problems, including the necessity of lying to the authorities, she could never fully understand what I was getting at. Her big, round eyes stopped sparkling in that happy face, and she said, "Look. Look. Who else would have taken care of them if we didn't? They needed our help, and they needed it *then.*"[18]

As impulses, kindness and goodness may not be explainable in rational terms. While it is not dangerous under normal circumstances, kindness is almost always inconvenient. The word derives from the Old English *cynd,* pertaining to race, family, or kin.[19] Within our families, we may willingly go out of our way to be helpful, while outside this boundary we may think twice about expending any effort. There may seem to be nothing to gain from being generous with our time or talents beyond our immediate circle.

Yet kindness is most moving and meaningful precisely when it is rendered by those who are not kin, or in the absence of something to gain. In *The Altruistic Personality,* Samuel Oliner and Pearl Oliner present the results of extensive interviews both with people who rescued Jews in Nazi Europe and with those who chose not be rescuers: "What distinguished rescuers was . . . their stronger sense of attachment to others and their feeling of responsibility for the welfare of others, including those outside their immediate familial or communal circles."[20]

A twenty-eight-year-old woman recalls two instances of encountering kindness from strangers:

One time when I was traveling in India I lost my backpack. All my clothes and things were in there. I felt totally vulnerable, at the mercy of strangers whose language I couldn't speak. Then a woman loaned me her own clothes. You can't imagine how grateful I felt. It was the same way here when I got sick. I was in my own country, but I felt just like I did that time in India. I was in the hospital, far away from home, getting care from doctors I didn't know. I was scared and in pain. Then a lady from the dietary department started talking to me. She kept dropping by my room on the excuse of updating the menus. She'd crack jokes, tell me stories, make me laugh. She was the kindest person I'd ever met. She made me feel better in so many ways. You never forget things like that. Ever since then, I've been on the alert for lost people wherever I go. I know

what it means to run into a good person when you
need one.

What is most striking in accounts of kindness is its simplicity. One person notices the difficulty of another and
acts accordingly. In *The Possibility of Altruism,* Thomas Nagel
writes, "It is a question not of compassion but of simply
connecting, in order to see what one's attitudes commit one
to. Recognition of the other person's reality, and the possibility of putting yourself in his place, is essential."[21] Samuel
Schurgin, a Talmudic scholar, similarly suggests that an
"anticipatory alertness to the reactions, feelings and specu-
lations of others" is the essence of kindness. He cites this
example:

> When Rabbi Eliyahu Dov Lazerowitz (1856–1941) was
> once hurrying through the streets with his students to-
> ward the yeshiva, he suddenly slowed down to a snail's
> pace the moment he had noticed an elderly gentleman
> walking ahead with great strain. His students were puz-
> zled over the rabbi's sudden change of pace and ques-
> tioned him about it. "If we were to rush past that man,"
> he explained, "he might feel badly that he can no
> longer move as fast as we can."[22]

Heightened sensitivity toward the feelings of others is
exactly the change I have observed in people who have benefitted from such sensitivity. When it is most fruitful, kindness is passed on in the form of generosity toward others.
Jaded people who have lived only for themselves begin to
take an interest in those around them, having discovered
the worth of mercy through their own vulnerability. Bitter
people begin to experiment with nurturance, having tasted
something of its satisfactions when they were ill.

GENEROSITY AND HOPE

I once knew a hundred-year-old woman whose husband had died ten years earlier, precipitating a move to a nursing home. She had never had children and had outlived almost all of her friends. Her mother, father, and sister had died many decades ago. She was, for me, the embodiment of total aloneness. She had lived a full and generous life, yet had been unable to avoid being set adrift in her last years. It seemed that living a good life did not ensure a good ending.

As I came to know her better, this woman revealed to me that one of the aides on the night shift was "like a daughter" to her. They spoke intimately about their lives and looked forward to seeing each other as often as possible. When we were finally introduced, her friend told me:

> I'd do anything for her. She's been a help to me in so many ways. There she is, all gnarled up in her wheelchair, hardly able to move a muscle, and she moves mountains in my life. Her spirit is powerful, because she's just so interested in other people's lives. A lot of times I've come to work depressed, but spending a few minutes with her cheered me right up. It's her wit. She makes you laugh at yourself, and pretty soon you see things differently. She's lived such a long time that she doesn't take things seriously that bother a younger person. She's part of this world and out of this world at the same time. I hope I can be like her someday.

Many people wonder what they can do earlier in life to prepare for their eventual frailty. They scrutinize those who cope gracefully with illness and disability, trying to find out what distinguishes them from those who collapse in on themselves. A man with Parkinson's disease offers his reflections:

Among the many parkinsonians I know, there is little relationship between how happy a person is and his or her physical condition. Some who have only a slight tremor are bitter about their fate and continually ask "Why me?" Others, who are so debilitated they are confined to a wheelchair, are cheerful, gregarious, and concerned about others."[23]

From such observations, many conclude that our personality traits have a greater influence on our fate than do the particular deteriorations we endure. In *The Republic,* Plato ventures this proposition: "For if men are sensible and good-tempered, old age is easy enough to bear: if not, youth as well as age is a burden."[24] According to this reasoning, we are doomed or blessed by the accident of our natures. We can predict from our earlier manner of coping with hardship how we will react to our later losses.

Another view locates successful coping in our attitudes, or the degree to which we make up our minds to overcome obstacles. In *Living with Chronic Illness,* Cheri Register observes, "How well people manage their lives marked by illness depends not on the nature of the illness but on the strength of their conviction that life is worth living no matter what complications are imposed on it."[25] Blair Justice similarly argues in *Who Gets Sick* that "how we react is more important than is the fact that life can be hard or fraught with peril." He writes:

How aversive or damaging an event is depends on how we choose to take it—which means that we can control its effects on our bodies and health by our attitudes and beliefs . . . Some people are subjected to harsher circumstances than others are, such as through war, racism, poverty, unemployment or age. But . . . even under extreme conditions, it is possible not only to survive but to retain some sense of health and well-being.[26]

Other explanations look to our upbringing. In *Adaptation to Life,* George Vaillant claims that our responses to hardship are shaped in childhood. Parents who do not help their children cope with suffering leave them as adults with the "immature defenses" of denying their problems, distorting their role in them, or projecting the causes onto others. In contrast, parents who "stay with their children when they are upset" help them "learn the capacity to bear and plan for pain."[27]

There is both wisdom and untruth in each of these formulations. Our personality style and beliefs certainly influence our response to illness, but not irrevocably. Our experiences from childhood affect our later coping styles, but not in so linear a fashion. Some people raised under neglectful circumstances manage to garner enough strength to lead satisfying lives, and some raised under supportive conditions waste years through addictions and other detours away from their original aims.

In my clinical practice, I have observed that people with a history of generous exchanges with others tend to carry these inclinations with them to the end of their lives. Wherever they live, whatever they do, they readily make connections with other people and derive satisfaction from doing so. When frailty encroaches, they tend to be surrounded by loyal helpers. There can be no certain formula for security, but kindness is rarely wasted and the habit of generosity almost always serves as a strength.

The notion of detachment in old age is both accurate and misleading. For years, gerontologists have studied this tendency, questioning its prevalence and debating whether it is a sound or detrimental response to getting older. In *Growing Old: The Process of Disengagement,* one of the first studies, Elaine Cumming and William Henry examined a group of older people who were still healthy enough to maintain independent lives. They measured the numbers of people with whom this sample group had contact, as well as changes in the frequency of these encounters. They concluded that "aging is an inevitable mutual withdrawal or disengagement, resulting in decreased interaction between the aging person and others in the social systems he belongs to."[28]

Depending on how one chooses to measure disengagement, however, data can be marshalled to confirm or deny this conclusion. The answer is not clearly measurable, resting more in attitudes and feelings than in actions. The various meanings of detachment diverge widely, with some signifying a withdrawal from social contact and others indicating a lessened need for external assurances of one's worth. There are people who remain deeply involved in other people's lives yet who withdraw from the concerns of the wider world.

In his last years, Freud corresponded with Lou Andreas-Salome, a fellow psychoanalyst with whom he felt a particularly deep kinship. In one letter, he wrote:

> A crust of indifference is slowly creeping up around me; a fact I state without complaining. It is a natural development, a way of beginning to grow inorganic. The "detachment of old age", I think it is called. . . . The change taking place is perhaps not very noticeable; everything is an interesting as it was before, neither are the ingredients very different; but some kind of resonance is lacking; unmusical as I am, I imagine

the difference to be something like using the pedal or not.[29]

Detachment that springs out of a sense of removal from previous ambitions and projects may give us more room for generosity and intimacy, rather than less. An inner spaciousness may arise in which involvement in the lives of other people is given more prominence, since other concerns no longer crowd out this impulse.

No matter what our personality, beliefs, or upbringing, the approach of death may prompt us to revise our conduct in terms of this awareness. In *Sowings and Reapings*, Andrew Schmookler contends that we cannot alter the circumstances that shaped us, but we can affect the way we live in the present. He writes, "What the world sows in us may grow into aspects of who we are, but some aspects may predominate over others. . . . Our destiny, therefore, depends on which part of our character we allow to govern our destiny."[30]

A woman in her late thirties once told me why she was devoting every Saturday morning to doing chores for an elderly neighbor who had no family:

> Look, this could easily be me someday, living alone in a tiny apartment, trying to make ends meet with my social security check. All it takes is something to go wrong with your heart or your shoulder, and you can't carry your groceries any more or handle a vacuum cleaner. This gives me hope that someone like me will be around when it's my turn.

The belief that there will be people around to assist us during our time of need is the conviction that we create by our own example. Acting in a right manner reassures us, as if every act of goodness we perform goes into the human

pool. We see firsthand that individual efforts can indeed reduce suffering and that not all hardships are beyond
human control.

§

The expectation that we will be able to count on kindness during our time of need becomes one of life's most sus-
taining convictions. We hope that if we become incapacitated, our friends and relatives will stand by us. We hope
that their help will arise out of affection rather than out of
pity, and that we will bear our difficulties gracefully enough
to keep on inspiring their loyalty. We suspect that the measure of a good life is how we are treated at the end.

Notes

Preface

1. Martin Tolchin, "When Long Life Is Too Much: Suicide Rises Among Elderly," *The New York Times*, July 19, 1989, p. 1.
2. Ludwig Wittgenstein, *Philosophical Investigations* (New York: The Macmillan Company, 1958), 15.
3. Alice M. Rivlin and Joshua M. Wiener, *Caring for the Disabled Elderly: Who Will Pay?* (Washington, D.C.: The Brookings Institution, 1988), 5.

ONE *A Desert of Time*

1. Florida Scott-Maxwell, *The Measure of My Days* (New York: Penguin Books, 1979), 41.
2. May Sarton, *The House by the Sea* (New York: W. W. Norton and Company, 1977), 27.
3. Kathleen Fischer, *Winter Grace: Spirituality for the Later Years* (New York: Paulist Press, 1985), 24.
4. Alan H. Olmstead, *Threshold: The First Days of Retirement* (New York: Harper and Row, 1975), 176–77.
5. Alan H. Olmstead, pp. 180–81.
6. Ruth Howard Gray, *Survival of the Spirit: My Detour Through a Retirement Home* (Atlanta: John Knox Press, 1985), 39.
7. Eviatar Zerubavel, *The Seven Day Circle: The History and Meaning of the Week* (New York: The Free Press, 1985), 106, 120.
8. Robert L. Rubinstein, *Singular Paths: Old Men Living Alone* (New York: Columbia University Press, 1986), 100.

181

9. Harriet Robey, *There's a Dance in the Old Dame Yet* (Boston: Little, Brown and Company, 1982), 47.

10. Harriet Robey, pp. 47, 48.

11. Thomas Mann, *The Magic Mountain* (New York: Vintage Books, 1969), 104–5.

12. This passage from "Gifts" in *The Complete Works of Ralph Waldo Emerson* is quoted by James D. Wallace in *Virtues and Vices* (Ithaca: Cornell University Press, 1978), 154.

13. Barbara Myerhoff, *Number Our Days* (New York: Simon and Schuster, 1978), 263.

14. Aleksandr Solzhenitsyn, *The Gulag Archipelago* (New York: Harper and Row, 1973), I-II, 591–92.

15. Virginia Woolf, *Moments of Being* (New York: Harcourt Brace Jovanovich, 1978), 70.

16. Mario Milletti, *Voices of Experience: 1500 Retired People Talk About Retirement* (New York: Teachers Insurance and Annuity Association College Retirement Equities Fund, 1984), 118.

17. William Shakespeare, *Much Ado About Nothing*, act 5, scene 4.

18. Michael Drury, *Counter-Clock-Wise: Reflections of a Maverick* (New York: Walker Publishing Company, 1987), 48.

19. Malcolm Cowley, *The View from 80* (New York: The Viking Press, 1976), 12.

20. Robert L. Rubinstein, p. 32.

21. Odell Shepard, Ed., *The Heart of Thoreau's Journals* (New York: Dover Publications, 1961), 100–101.

22. Philip Hallie, *Lest Innocent Blood Be Shed* (New York: Harper Colophon Books, 1979), 276.

TWO *The Quality of Mercy*

1. Aristotle, *Nicomachean Ethics* (Indianapolis: The Bobbs-Merrill Company, 1962), 50.

2. William Morris, Ed., *The American Heritage Dictionary* (New York: American Heritage Publishing Company, 1969), 821 and 1529.

3. Nancy Mairs, *Plain Text* (Tucson: The University of Arizona Press, 1986), 15.

4. James J. Dowd, "Aging as Exchange: A Preface to Theory," *Journal of Gerontology,* Vol. 30, No. 5, 1975, pp. 587–90.

5. Jo Ann Miller, "The Sandwich Generation," *Working Mother,* January 1987, p. 48.

6. Ronald Blythe, *The View in Winter: Reflections on Old Age* (New York: Harcourt Brace Jovanovich, 1979), 119.

7. Tacitus, *The Annals of Imperial Rome* (Baltimore: Penguin Books, 1956), 162.

8. Ruth Benedict, *The Chrysanthemum and the Sword* (Boston: Houghton Mifflin Company, 1946), 104–6.

9. Donald M. Frame, Trans., *The Complete Essays of Montaigne* (Stanford: Stanford University Press, 1973), 612.

10. Excerpts from the writings of William Posner are quoted by Mary Buckley in *The Aged Are People, Too* (Port Washington, N.Y.: Kennikat Press, 1972), 79.

11. James D. Wallace, *Virtues and Vices* (Ithaca: Cornell University Press, 1978), 156.

12. Barbara Myerhoff, *Number Our Days* (New York: Simon and Schuster, 1978), 268.

13. Barbara Myerhoff, "Surviving Stories: Reflections on 'Number Our Days,' " *Tikkun,* Vol. 2, No. 5, November/December 1987, p. 20.

14. Leon Roth, *Judaism: A Portrait* (New York: The Viking Press, 1960), 24.

15. Ruth Howard Gray, *Survival of the Spirit: My Detour Through A Retirement Home* (Atlanta: John Knox Press, 1985), 34.

16. Ruth Howard Gray, p. 38.

17. William James, *Essays in Pragmatism* (New York: Hafner Publishing Company, 1957), 78.

THREE *Bodily Terms*

1. Albert Memmi, *Dependence* (Boston: Beacon Press, 1984), 3.

2. Virginia Woolf, *The Moment and Other Essays* (New York: Harcourt Brace Jovanovich, 1974), 9.

3. Arthur Kleinman, *The Illness Narratives: Suffering, Healing, and the Human Condition* (New York: Basic Books, 1988), 29.

4. Derived from "Riding the Gale," a documentary about a New Zealand woman adapting to multiple sclerosis. Produced by Genni and Kim Batterham. Distributed by Filmmakers Library, Inc., 124 East 40th St., New York, NY 10016.

5. Audre Lorde, *The Cancer Journals* (San Francisco: Spinsters / Aunt Lute, 1980), 15.

6. Martha Cleveland, *Living Well: A Twelve-Step Response to Chronic Illness and Disability* (San Francisco: Harper and Row, 1989), 18.

7. Andrew Malcolm, *This Far and No More* (New York: New American Library, 1987), 75.

8. Martha Weinman Lear, *Heartsounds* (New York: Pocket Books, 1980), 379.

9. Ruth Pinder, "Striking Balances: Living with Parkinson's Disease," in *Living with Chronic Illness* (London: Unwin Hyman, 1988), 78.

10. Ida Daly, *Adventure in a Wheelchair* (Philadelphia: Whitmore Publishing Company, 1973), 71.

11. Charles E. Eaton, "Ripening Past Despair," in Phillip L. Berman, Ed., *The Courage to Grow Old* (New York: Ballantine Books, 1989), 80–81.

12. Norman Cousins, *Anatomy of an Illness as Perceived by the Patient* (New York: Bantam Books, 1981), 72–73.

13. May Sarton, *After the Stroke* (New York: W. W. Norton and Company, 1988), 97, 125.

14. Susan Schnur, "Hers," *The New York Times,* July 26, 1985.

15. Ruth Howard Gray, *Survival of the Spirit: My Detour Through a Retirement Home* (Atlanta: John Knox Press, 1985), 81.

16. Albert Camus, *The Myth of Sisyphus* (New York: Vintage Books, 1955), 6–7.

17. Harriet Robey, *There's a Dance in the Old Dame Yet* (Boston: Little, Brown and Company, 1982), 123.

18. Elizabeth Bishop, *Geography III* (New York: Farrar, Straus, and Giroux, 1976), 40.

19. Madeleine L'Engle, *The Summer of the Great-Grandmother* (New York: The Seabury Press, 1979), 19–20.

20. Norman O. Brown, *Life Against Death: The Psychoanalytical Meaning of History* (Middletown, Conn.: Wesleyan University Press, 1970), 293.

21. Oliver Sacks, *A Leg to Stand On* (New York: Harper and Row, 1987), 202–3.

22. Ivan Illich, *Medical Nemesis: The Expropriation of Health* (New York: Pantheon Books, 1976), 132.

23. Jack Weinberg, "What Do I Say to My Mother When I Have Nothing to Say?" in Steven Steury and Marie L. Blank, Eds., *Readings in Psychotherapy with Older People* (Rockville, Md.: National Institute of Mental Health, 1978), 228.

24. Sallie Tisdale, "Dancing in the Wind," in Jessica Bryan, Ed., *Love is Ageless: Stories About Alzheimer's Disease* (Oakland, Calif.: Serala Press, 1987), 37.

25. Maurice Lamm, *The Jewish Way in Death and Mourning* (New York: Jonathan David Publishers, 1969), 136–37.

26. Mark Pelgrin, *And a Time to Die* (Sausalito, Calif.: Angel Island Publications, 1962), 12.

27. William Wharton, *Dad* (New York: Avon Books, 1981), 144–45.

28. Paul Monette, *Borrowed Time* (New York: Harcourt Brace Jovanovich, 1988), 43.

29. Doris Lund, *Eric* (New York: Dell Publishing Company, 1974), 246.

FOUR *The Worth of the Past*

1. William Morris, Ed., *The American Heritage Dictionary* (New York: American Heritage Publishing Company, 1969), 273, 1104.

2. George D. Painter, *Marcel Proust: A Biography* (New York: Vintage Books, 1978), Vol. I, xiii.

3. E. B. White, *Essays of E. B. White* (New York: Harper Colophon Books, 1977), 3–4.

4. Gretel Ehrlich, *The Solace of Open Spaces* (New York: Penguin Books, 1985), 25.

5. Walter Benjamin, *Illuminations* (New York: Schocken Books, 1969), 67, 42.

6. Frances Yates, *The Art of Memory* (Chicago: The University of Chicago Press, 1966), 3.

7. Thomas Mallon, *A Book of One's Own: People and Their Diaries* (New York: Penguin Books, 1984), xv.

8. Paul Auster, *The Invention of Solitude* (New York: Avon Books, 1982), 10–11, 13.

9. Rainer Maria Rilke, *Duino Elegies* (New York: W. W. Norton and Company, 1963), 71.

10. Robert Grudin, *Time and the Art of Living* (New York: Ticknor and Fields, 1982), 183.

11. Rainer Maria Rilke, *Letters to a Young Poet* (New York: W. W. Norton, 1954), 20.

12. Dorothea S. Greenbaum, "Elderly, Then Old," *The New York Times,* December 9, 1985.

13. Robert L. Rubinstein, *Singular Paths: Old Men Living Alone* (New York: Columbia University Press, 1986), 89.

14. Peter G. Coleman, *Ageing and Reminiscence Processes* (New York: John Wiley and Sons, 1986), 110–11.

15. Sigmund Freud, "Recollection, Repetition and Working Through," in *Therapy and Technique* (New York: Collier Books, 1963), 160.

16. Marc Kaminsky, Ed., *The Uses of Reminiscence: New Ways of Working with Older Adults* (New York: The Haworth Press, 1984), 18.

17. Viktor Frankl, *Man's Search for Meaning* (New York: Pocket Books, 1963), 192.

18. Victor Zuckerkandl, *The Sense of Music* (Princeton: Princeton University Press, 1959), 27, 87.

19. Peter Brooks, *Reading for the Plot: Design and Intention in Narrative* (New York: Random House, 1985), 99–100.

20. Erving Polster, *Every Person's Life Is Worth a Novel* (New York: W. W. Norton and Company, 1987), 10, 32.

21. Frank Kermode, *The Sense of an Ending* (New York: Oxford University Press, 1968), 57–59.

22. Sharon R. Kaufman, *The Ageless Self: Sources of Meaning in Late Life* (New York: New American Library, 1986), 152.

23. Morton Lieberman and Sheldon Tobin, *The Experience of Old Age: Stress, Coping, and Survival* (New York: Basic Books, 1983), 309.

24. Hannah Arendt, *The Human Condition* (Chicago: The University of Chicago Press, 1973), 97.

25. Anonymous, "Death in the First Person," in Elisabeth Kübler-Ross, *Death: The Final Stage of Growth* (Englewood Cliffs, N.J.: Prentice-Hall, 1975), 26.

26. Doris Kearns, "Angles of Vision," in Marc Pachter, Ed., *Telling Lives: The Biographer's Art* (Philadelphia: University of Pennsylvania Press, 1981), 100–101.

FIVE   *Parents Dying*

1. Bonnie Bluh, *The "Old" Speak Out* (New York: Horizon Press, 1979), 202.

2. Norbert Elias, *The Loneliness of the Dying* (New York: Basil Blackwell, 1985), 69–70.

3. Gerald Blidstein, *Honor Thy Father and Mother: Filial Responsibility in Jewish Law and Ethics* (New York: Ktav Publishing House, 1975), 119.

4. Lee Headley, *Adults and Their Parents in Family Therapy* (New York: Plenum Press, 1977), 47.

5. Phillip Moffitt, "The Power of One Woman," in Scott Walker, Ed., *The Graywolf Annual Three: Essays, Memoirs and Reflections* (St. Paul, Minn.: Graywolf Press, 1986), 50–51.

6. John Kotre, *Outliving the Self: Generativity and the Interpretation of Lives* (Baltimore: The Johns Hopkins University Press, 1984), 21–22.

7. Jane Norris, Ed., *Daughters of the Elderly: Building Partnerships in Caregiving* (Bloomington: Indiana University Press, 1988), 12, 14.

8. Ivan Boszormenyi-Nagy and Geraldine Spark, *Invisible Loyalties: Reciprocity in Intergenerational Family Therapy* (Hagerstown, Md.: Harper and Row, 1973), 228.

9. Rabbi Avrohom Chaim Feuer, *The Ten Commandments: A New Translation with a Commentary Anthologized from Talmudic, Midrashic, and Rabbinic Sources* (New York: Mesorah Publications, 1986), 52.

10. Keith Vacha, *Quiet Fire: Memoirs of Older Gay Men* (Trumansburg, N.Y.: The Crossing Press, 1985), 10.

11. Takeo Doi, *The Anatomy of Dependence* (Tokyo: Kodansha International, 1973), 62, 122.

12. William Morris, Ed., *The American Heritage Dictionary* (New York: American Heritage Publishing Company, 1969), 1096, 1518.

13. Karen Horney, *The Adolescent Diaries of Karen Horney* (New York: Basic Books, 1980), 265.

14. Yasushi Inoue, *Chronicle of My Mother* (Tokyo: Kodansha International, 1982), 20–21.

15. Marc D. Angel, *The Orphaned Adult: Confronting the Death of a Parent* (New York: Human Sciences Press, 1987), 78.

16. Jane Norris, Ed., p. 68.

17. David J. Maitland, *Against the Grain: Coming Through Mid-Life Crisis* (New York: The Pilgrim Press, 1981), 149.

18. Madeleine L'Engle, *The Summer of the Great-Grandmother* (New York: The Seabury Press, 1979), 107.

19. Jane Howard, *A Different Woman* (New York: E. P. Dutton, 1973), 21.

20. Lily Pincus, *Death and the Family: The Importance of Mourning* (New York: Schocken Books, 1974), 232, 211.

21. C. G. Jung, *Memories, Dreams, Reflections* (New York: Vintage Books, 1963), 96.

22. Anna Quindlen, *Living Out Loud* (New York: Ivy Books, 1988), xvii.

23. Alice Bloch, *Lifetime Guarantee: A Journey Through Loss and Survival* (Watertown, Mass.: Persephone Press, 1981), 126, 128.

24. Madeleine L'Engle, pp. 50–51.

25. Edward Myers, *When Parents Die: A Guide for Adults* (New York: Penguin Books, 1986), 103–4.

26. May Sarton, *After the Stroke* (New York: W. W. Norton and Company, 1988), 15.

27. Violet Weingarten, *Intimations of Mortality* (New York: Alfred A. Knopf, 1978), 79.

28. Muriel Spark, *Memento Mori* (New York: Avon Books, 1973), 157.

29. Irvin D. Yalom, *Love's Executioner and Other Tales of Psychotherapy* (New York: Basic Books, 1989), 86.

30. Erik Erikson, *Identity and the Life Cycle* (New York: W. W. Norton and Company, 1980), 104.

SIX   *Unlived Life*

1. Excerpts from the writings of William Posner are quoted by Mary Buckley in *The Aged Are People, Too* (Port Washington, N.Y.: Kennikat Press, 1972), 31, 36.

2. Sally Gadow, "Frailty and Strength: The Dialectic of Aging," in Thomas R. Cole and Sally Gadow, Eds., *What Does It Mean to Grow Old? Reflections from the Humanities* (Durham, N.C.: Duke University Press, 1986), 243.

3. Margaret Huyck, *Growing Older: Things You Need to Know About Aging* (Englewood Cliffs, N.J.: Prentice-Hall, 1974), xii.

4. Robert C. Cantor, *And a Time to Live: Toward Emotional Well-Being During the Crisis of Cancer* (New York: Harper Colophon Books, 1978), 94.

5. Lewis Mumford, *The Conduct of Life* (New York: Harcourt Brace Jovanovich, 1970), 255–57.

6. Laura Chester, *Lupus Novice: Toward Self-Healing* (Barrytown, N.Y.: Station Hill Press, 1987), 49, 50, 67.

7. Virginia Woolf, *Moments of Being* (New York: Harcourt Brace Jovanovich, 1978), 98.

8. Max Picard, *The World of Silence* (Washington, D.C.: Regnery Gateway, 1988), 18–19.

9. Donald M. Frame, Trans., *The Complete Essays of Montaigne* (Stanford: Stanford University Press, 1973), 576.

10. Irvin D. Yalom, *Existential Psychotherapy* (New York: Basic Books, 1980), 37.

11. David Gutmann, *Reclaimed Powers: Toward a New Psychology of Men and Women in Later Life* (New York: Basic Books, 1987), 250.

12. William James, *The Varieties of Religious Experience: A Study in Human Nature* (London: Longmans, Green and Company, 1929), 212.

13. William James, p. 214.

14. Paul Tournier, *Learn to Grow Old* (San Francisco: Harper and Row, 1983), 118–19.

15. Alfed Adler, *What Life Should Mean to You* (New York: Perigee Books, 1980), 13.

16. Immanuel Kant, *Foundations of the Metaphysics of Morals* (New York: The Bobbs-Merrill Company, 1959), 14–15, 41.

17. Robert F. Murphy, *The Body Silent* (New York: Henry Holt and Company, 1987), 42–43.

18. Jerome Ellison, *The Last Third of Life Club* (Philadelphia: Pilgrim Press, 1973), 150.

19. M. C. Richards, *Centering: In Pottery, Poetry, and the Person* (Middletown, Conn.: Wesleyan University Press, 1972), 35.

20. Barbara Macdonald, *Look Me in the Eye: Old Women, Aging and Ageism* (San Francisco: Spinsters, Ink, 1983), 108.

21. Wayne A. Myers, *Dynamic Therapy of the Older Patient* (New York: Jason Aronson, 1984), 185, 182.

22. Robert C. Peck, "Psychological Developments in the Second Half of Life," in Bernice L. Neugarten, Ed., *Middle Age and Aging: A Reader in Social Psychology* (Chicago: The University of Chicago Press, 1968), 89.

23. Ronald Blythe, *The View in Winter: Reflections on Old Age* (New York: Harcourt Brace Jovanovich, 1979), 220.

24. James Hillman, *Suicide and the Soul* (New York: Harper Colophon Books, 1964), 164.

25. Ronald Blythe, p. 177.

26. Cicely Saunders, "The Moment of Truth: Care of the Dying Person," in Leonard Pearson, Ed., *Death and Dying: Current Issues in the Treatment of the Dying Person* (Cleveland: The Press of Case Western Reserve University, 1969), 78.

27. Donald Richie, Ed., *Ikiru: A Film by Akira Kurosawa* (New York: Simon and Schuster, 1968), 33–34.

28. Arthur Schopenhauer, "The Ages of Life," in Patrick L. McKee, Ed., *Philosophical Foundations of Gerontology* (New York: Human Sciences Press, 1982), 201.

29. Robert C. Cantor, p. 21.

30. Violet Weingarten, *Intimations of Mortality* (New York: Alfred A. Knopf, 1978), 6–7.

31. Jean-Jacques Rousseau, *Reveries of the Solitary Walker* (New York: Penguin Books, 1979), 137.

32. Paul Tsongas, *Heading Home* (New York: Alfred A. Knopf, 1984), 163.

33. Jean-Jacques Rousseau, p. 51.

SEVEN *Refusing to Be Demeaned*

1. Robert F. Murphy, *The Body Silent* (New York: Henry Holt and Company, 1987), 117.

2. John Gliedman and William Roth, *The Unexpected Minority: Handicapped Children in America* (New York: Harcourt Brace Jovanovich, 1980), 20.

3. Paul Starr, *The Social Transformation of American Medicine* (New York: Basic Books, 1982), 431.

4. Anne Scitovsky, "The High Cost of Dying: What Do the Data Show?" *Health and Society*, No. 66, 1984, 591–608.

5. Robert Miner, "Why Hospitals Make Mistakes," *Newsweek,* June 17, 1985, p. 21.

6. Charles E. Rosenberg, *The Care of Strangers* (New York: Basic Books, 1987), 10.

7. Arthur Kleinman, *The Illness Narratives: Suffering, Healing, and the Human Condition* (New York: Basic Books, 1988), 49, 52.

8. Keith A. Nichols, *Psychological Care in Physical Illness* (Philadelphia: The Charles Press, 1984), 31.

9. Norman Daniels, "Why Saying No to Patients in the U.S. Is So Hard," *The New England Journal of Medicine,* May 22, 1986, p. 1383.

10. Dieter Hessel, Ed., *Maggie Kuhn on Aging* (Philadelphia: The Westminster Press, 1977), 56–57.

11. Barbara D. Webster, *All of a Piece: A Life with Multiple Sclerosis* (Baltimore: The Johns Hopkins University Press, 1989), 68–73.

12. Marilynn J. Phillips, "Disability and Ethnicity in Conflict: A Study in Transformation," in Michelle Fine and Adrienne Asch, Eds., *Women with Disabilities: Essays in Psychology, Culture, and Politics* (Philadelphia: Temple University Press, 1988), 209.

13. Barbara Macdonald, *Look Me in the Eye: Old Women, Aging and Ageism* (San Francisco: Spinsters, Ink, 1983), 91–92.

14. Simone de Beauvoir, *The Coming of Age* (New York: Warner Books, 1973), 420.

15. Alex Comfort, *A Good Age* (New York: Simon and Schuster, 1976), 23.

16. John Gliedman and William Roth, p. 21.

17. Fred Davis, "Deviance Disavowal: The Management of Strained Interaction by the Visibly Handicapped," in Howard S. Becker, Ed., *The Other Side: Perspectives on Deviance* (New York: The Free Press, 1967), 129.

18. Fred Davis, p. 128.

19. Robert C. Cantor, *And a Time to Live: Toward Emotional Well-Being During the Crisis of Cancer* (New York: Harper Colophon Books, 1978), 15.

20. Barbara D. Webster, p. 108.

21. Robert F. Murphy, p. 109.

22. Theodor Reik, *Listening with the Third Ear: The Inner Experience of a Psychoanalyst* (New York: Farrar, Straus and Giroux, 1983), 173.

23. Carolyn Hardesty, "Pain," in Marsha Saxton and Florence Howe, Eds., *With Wings: An Anthology of Literature by and about Women with Disabilities* (New York: The Feminist Press at The City University of New York, 1987), 23.

24. Erving Goffman, *Stigma: Notes on the Management of Spoiled Identity* (Englewood Cliffs, N.J.: Prentice-Hall, 1963), 42.

25. Berenice Fisher and Roberta Galler, "Friendship and Fairness:

How Disability Affects Friendship Between Women," in Michelle Fine and Adrienne Asch, Eds., *Women with Disabilities: Essays in Psychology, Culture, and Politics* (Philadelphia: Temple University Press, 1988), 183–84.

26. Violet Weingarten, *Intimations of Mortality* (New York: Alfred A. Knopf, 1978), 12.

27. Elaine Starkman, "Mother-in-Law Diary," in Lyn Lifshin, Ed., *Ariadne's Thread: A Collection of Contemporary Women's Journals* (New York: Harper and Row, 1982), 229.

28. Frederick Douglass, *The Life and Times of Frederick Douglass* (New York: Collier Books, 1962), 143.

29. Erving Goffman, p. 118.

30. Irving Kenneth Zola, *Missing Pieces: A Chronicle of Living with a Disability* (Philadelphia: Temple University Press, 1982), 226.

31. Irving Kenneth Zola, p. 206.

EIGHT *The Fiction of Independence*

1. Paul Monette, *Borrowed Time* (New York: Harcourt Brace Jovanovich, 1988), 282.

2. Eric J. Cassell, "Dying in a Technological Society," in Peter Steinfels and Robert M. Veatch, Eds., *Death Inside Out: The Hastings Center Report* (New York: Harper and Row, 1975), 45.

3. Thomas Bender, *Community and Social Change in America* (Baltimore: The Johns Hopkins University Press, 1982), 108, 93.

4. Helena Z. Lopata, *Widowhood in an American City* (Cambridge, Mass.: Schenkman Publishing Company, 1973), 236, 228, 227.

5. Ronald Gross, Beatrice Gross, and Sylvia Seidman, Eds., *The New Old: Struggling for Decent Aging* (Garden City, N.Y.: Anchor Books, 1978), 268, 270–71.

6. Rachel Z. Dulin, *A Crown of Glory: A Biblical View of Aging* (New York: Paulist Press, 1988), 106–7.

7. Andrew J. Cherlin and Frank F. Furstenberg, Jr., *The New American Grandparent: A Place in the Family, A Life Apart* (New York: Basic Books, 1986), 197–98.

8. Nancy Foner, *Ages in Conflict: A Cross-Cultural Perspective on Inequality Between Old and Young* (New York: Columbia University Press, 1984), 110.

9. Mark H. Ingraham, *My Purpose Holds: Reactions and Experiences in Retirement of TIAA-CREF Annuitants* (New York: Teachers Insurance and Annuity Association, 1974), 106.

10. Thomas H. Johnson and Theodora Ward, Eds., *The Letters of Emily Dickinson* (Cambridge, Mass.: The Belknap Press, 1958), 843.

11. Sharon R. Kaufman, *The Ageless Self* (New York: New American Library, 1986), 110.

12. Mark H. Ingraham, p. 31.

13. Barbara Myerhoff, *Number Our Days* (New York: Simon and Schuster, 1978), 253.

14. Mark H. Ingraham, pp. 31–32.

15. Angela Livingstone, *Salome: Her Life and Work* (Mt. Kisco, N.Y.: Moyer Bell, 1984), 202.

16. Lewis Hyde, *The Gift: Imagination and the Erotic Life of Property* (New York: Vintage Books, 1979), 20–21.

17. Arlie Russell Hochschild, *The Unexpected Community: Portrait of an Old Age Subculture* (Berkeley: University of California Press, 1978), 70, 72.

18. William Morris, Ed., *The American Heritage Dictionary* (New York: American Heritage Publishing Company, Inc., 1969), 549–50, 1516.

19. Martin E. P. Seligman, *Helplessness: On Depression, Development, and Death* (San Francisco: W. H. Freeman and Company, 1975), 98–99.

20. Erving Goffman, *Stigma: Notes on the Management of Spoiled Identity* (Englewood Cliffs, N.J.: Prentice-Hall, 1963), 119.

21. Beverly S. Gordon, *The First Year Alone* (Dublin, N.H.: William L. Bauhan, Publisher, 1986), 78.

22. Richard J. Margolis, *Risking Old Age in America* (Boulder, Colo.: Westview Press, 1990), 103.

23. Robertson Davies, *One Half of Robertson Davies* (New York: Penguin Books, 1977), 65, 64.

24. Robert Henri, *The Art Spirit* (Philadelphia: J. B. Lippincott Company, 1960), 220.

25. Robert Kegan, *The Evolving Self: Problems and Process in Human Development* (Cambridge, Mass.: Harvard University Press, 1982), 108, 107.

26. Richard J. Margolis, p. 116.

NINE *Prospects for Revival*

1. Alan Jabbour, "Some Thoughts from a Folk Cultural Perspective," in Priscilla W. Johnston, Ed., *Perspectives on Aging: Exploding the Myths* (Cambridge, Mass.: Ballinger Publishing Company, 1981), 144.

2. Mary Hufford, Marjorie Hunt, and Steven Zeitlin, *The Grand Generation: Memory, Mastery, Legacy* (Washington, D.C.: Smithsonian Institution, 1987), 70.

3. Lawrence LeShan and Eda LeShan, "Psychotherapy and the Pa-

tient with a Limited Life-Span," in Hendrik M. Ruitenbeek, Ed., *Death: Interpretations* (New York: Dell Publishing Company, 1969), 109, 113.

4. Maxwell Jones, *Growing Old—The Ultimate Freedom* (New York: Human Sciences Press, 1988), 17–18.

5. Lucille Wolfe, "A Kind of Odyssey," in Marc Kaminsky, Ed., *The Uses of Reminiscence: New Ways of Working with Older Adults* (New York: The Haworth Press, 1984), 216.

6. Michael Drury, *Counter-Clock-Wise: Reflections of a Maverick* (New York: Walker Publishing Company, 1987), 88–91.

7. Mark H. Ingraham, *My Purpose Holds: Reactions and Experiences in Retirement of TIAA-CREF Annuitants* (New York: Teachers Insurance and Annuity Association, 1974), 109.

8. Jules Z. Willing, *The Reality of Retirement: The Inner Experience of Becoming a Retired Person* (New York: William Morrow and Company, 1981), 77.

9. George A. Kelly, *A Theory of Personality: The Psychology of Personal Constructs* (New York: W. W. Norton and Company, 1963), 128–29.

10. Robert E. Van Rosen, *Comeback: The Story of My Stroke* (New York: The Bobbs-Merrill Company, 1963), 53.

11. Barbara D. Webster, *All of a Piece: A Life with Multiple Sclerosis* (Baltimore: The Johns Hopkins University Press, 1989), 34.

12. Joan Kelley, "Seniors Talk About Why They Volunteer," *Generations*, Vol. V., No. 4, Summer 1981, p. 18–19.

13. Bonnie Bluh, *The "Old" Speak Out* (New York: Horizon Press, 1979), 11.

14. Ben Weininger and Eva L. Menkin, *Aging is a Lifelong Affair* (Santa Barbara: Ross-Erickson, 1978), 9, 17.

15. Mary Hufford, Marjorie Hunt, and Steven Zeitlin, *The Grand Generation: Memory, Mastery, and Legacy* (Washington, D.C.: Smithsonian Institution, 1987), 27–28.

16. Mark H. Ingraham, p. 108.

17. Sidney Dorros, *Parkinson's: A Patient's View* (Cabin Johns, Md.: Seven Locks Press, 1981), 131.

18. Ashley Montagu, *Growing Young* (Granby, Massachusetts: Bergin and Garvey Publishers, 1989), 175.

19. Jim Heynen, *One Hundred Over 100: Moments with One Hundred North American Centenarians* (Golden, Colo.: Fulcrum Publishing, 1990), 83.

20. Norman Cousins, *Anatomy of an Illness as Perceived by the Patient* (New York: Bantam Books, 1981), 39.

21. Raymond Moody, Jr., *Laugh After Laugh: The Healing Power of Humor* (Jacksonville, Fla.: Headwaters Press, 1978), 21, 115.

22. Arthur Schopenhauer, *Studies in Pessimism: A Series of Essays* (St. Clair Shores, Mich.: Scholarly Press, 1968), 21.

23. Ingmar Bergman, *Fanny and Alexander* (New York: Pantheon Books, 1982), 207–8.

24. Lao Tzu, *Tao Teh Ching: The Way of Ways* (New York: Schocken Books, 1985), 65.

25. Stephen Crites, "Continuities: View from a Victorian Porch," *Soundings,* Fall 1973, pp. 261–63.

26. Emily Carr, *Hundreds and Thousands: The Journals of Emily Carr* (Toronto: Clarke, Irwin, and Company, 1978), 151.

27. Charles Taylor, Ed., *Growing On: Ideas About Aging* (New York: Van Nostrand Company, 1984), 112.

28. Cynthia Shaw Glasscock, "Rudolf Arnheim," *Michigan Today,* February 8, 1989, pp. 8–10.

29. Michael Drury, p. 8.

30. Barbara Macdonald, *Look Me in the Eye: Old Women, Aging and Ageism* (San Francisco: Spinsters, Ink, 1983), 18–19.

31. Robert L. Rubinstein, *Singular Paths: Old Men Living Alone* (New York: Columbia University Press, 1986), 25.

32. Betty Donley Harris, "I Write in Order to Live," in Jo Alexander, Debi Berrow, Lisa Domitrovich, Margarita Donnelly, and Cheryl McLean Eds., *Women and Aging: An Anthology by Women* (Corvallis, Oreg.: Calyx Books, 1986), 82–83.

33. Lillian B. Rubin, *Women of a Certain Age: The Midlife Search for Self* (New York: Harper and Row, 1979), 1.

34. Robert L. Rubinstein, pp. 170–71.

35. Robert N. Butler, "The Life Review: An Interpretation of Reminiscence in the Aged," in Patrick L. McKee, Ed., *Philosophical Foundations of Gerontology* (New York: Human Sciences Press, 1982), 238.

36. Mary Hufford, Marjorie Hunt, and Steven Zeitlin, *The Grand Generation: Memory, Mastery, Legacy* (Washington, D.C.: Smithsonian Institution, 1987), 42.

37. Anthony Storr, *Solitude: A Return to the Self* (New York: The Free Press, 1988), 194.

38. Elizabeth Yates, *Call It Zest: The Vital Ingredient After Seventy* (Brattleboro, Vt.: The Stephen Green Press, 1977), 27.

39. Jim Heynen, p. 45.

40. Francis O'Connor, "Albert Berne and the Completion of Being: Images of Vitality and Extinction in the Last Paintings of a Ninety-Six-Year-Old Man," in David D. Van Tassel, Ed., *Aging, Death, and the Completion of Being* (Philadelphia: University of Pennsylvania Press, 1979), 255.

CONCLUSION *The Measure of a Good Life*

1. Anatole Broyard, "Good Books About Being Sick," *The New York Times Book Review,* April 1, 1990, p. 1.

2. Albert B. Paine, Ed., *Mark Twain's Notebook* (New York: Harper and Brothers Publishers, 1935), 380.

3. Robert J. Kastenbaum, Theodore X. Barber, Sheryl C. Wilson, Beverly L. Ryder, and Lisa B. Hathaway, *Old, Sick, and Helpless: Where Therapy Begins* (Cambridge, Mass.: Ballinger Publishing Company, 1981), 4.

4. Philippe Aries, *The Hour of Our Death* (New York: Alfred A. Knopf, 1981), 560.

5. William Bridges, *Transitions* (Reading, Mass.: Addison-Wesley Publishing Company, 1980), 21.

6. Ken Wilber, *The Atman Project: A Transpersonal View of Human Development* (Wheaton, Ill.: The Theosophical Publishing House, 1980), 107.

7. Hannah Arendt, *The Human Condition* (Chicago: The University of Chicago Press, 1973), 126.

8. Robert N. Bellah, Richard Madsen, William M. Sullivan, Ann Swidler, and Steven M. Tipton, *Habits of the Heart* (New York: Harper and Row, 1985), vii.

9. David C. McClelland, *Power: The Inner Experience* (New York: Irvington Publishers, 1975), 85–86.

10. Carol Gilligan, *In a Different Voice: Psychological Theory and Women's Development* (Cambridge, Mass.: Harvard University Press, 1982), 156.

11. Ernest Becker, *The Denial of Death* (New York: The Free Press, 1973), 26.

12. Michael Novak, *The Experience of Nothingness* (New York: Harper and Row, 1978), 48.

13. Barbara Levy Simon, "Never-Married Old Women and Disability: A Majority Experience," in Michelle Fine and Adrienne Asch, Eds., *Women with Disabilities: Essays in Psychology, Culture, and Politics* (Philadelphia: Temple University Press, 1988), 222–23.

14. Lewis Thomas, *Late Night Thoughts on Listening to Mahler's Ninth Symphony* (New York: The Viking Press, 1983), 101, 105.

15. Robert C. Cantor, *And a Time to Live: Toward Emotional Well-Being During the Crisis of Cancer* (New York: Harper Colophon Books, 1978), 28.

16. Harvey A. Hornstein, *Cruelty and Kindness: A New Look at Aggression and Altruism* (Englewood Cliffs, N.J.: Prentice-Hall, 1976), 134.

17. Ben Weininger and Eva L. Menkin, *Aging is a Lifelong Affair* (Santa Barbara: Ross-Erikson, 1978), 20.

18. Philip Hallie, *Lest Innocent Blood Be Shed* (New York: Harper Colophon Books, 1979), 127.

19. William Morris, Ed., *The American Heritage Dictionary* (New York: American Heritage Publishing Company, 1969), 721, 1516.

20. Samuel P. Oliner and Pearl M. Oliner, *The Altruistic Personality: Rescuers of Jews in Nazi Europe* (New York: The Free Press, 1988), 249.

21. Thomas Nagel, *The Possibility of Altruism* (Princeton, New Jersey: Princeton University Press, 1970), 83.

22. Samuel B. Schurgin, *Chesed: The World Is Built Upon Kindness* (North Hollywood, Calif.: Netzach, 1985), 16.

23. Sidney Dorros, *Parkinson's: A Patient's View* (Cabin Johns, Md.: Seven Locks Press, 1981), 179.

24. Plato, *The Republic* (New York: Penguin Books, 1974), 63.

25. Cheri Register, *Living with Chronic Illness: Days of Patience and Passion* (New York: The Free Press, 1987), xiv.

26. Blair Justice, *Who Gets Sick: How Beliefs, Moods, and Thoughts Affect Your Health* (Los Angeles: Jeremy P. Tarcher, 1988), 23, 61–62.

27. George E. Vaillant, *Adaptation to Life* (Boston: Little, Brown and Company, 1977), 83, 160.

28. Elaine Cumming and William Henry, *Growing Old: The Process of Disengagement* (New York: Basic Books, 1961), 14.

29. Ernst Pfeiffer, *Sigmund Freud and Lou Andreas-Salome: Letters* (New York: W. W. Norton and Company, 1966), 154.

30. Andrew Bard Schmookler, *Sowings and Reapings: The Cycling of Good and Evil in the Human System* (Indianapolis: Knowledge Systems, Inc., 1989), 102.

Name Index

197

Subject Index